VEGAS STRONG

VEGAS STRONG

Bearing Witness
1 October 2017

Edited by

ROBERTA SABBATH

UNIVERSITY OF NEVADA PRESS | *Reno & Las Vegas*

Funded in part by a grant from Nevada Humanities,
and the National Endowment for the Humanities.

University of Nevada Press | Reno, Nevada 89557 USA
www.unpress.nevada.edu
Manufactured in the United States of America
FIRST PRINTING
Jacket design by Louise OFarrell; photograph ©gettyimages/Candace Stevens/EyeEm

Library of Congress Cataloging-in-Publication Data on file at lccn.loc.gov/2022036483
ISBN 978-1-64779-100-1 (cloth); ISBN 978-1-64779-101-8 (ebook)

The paper used in this book meets the requirements of American National Standard for
Information Sciences—Permanence of Paper for Printed Library Materials, ANSI/NISO
Z39.48–1992 (R2002).

~ For our children ~

Lives Lost

*The fifty-eight individuals who died from their
injuries in the immediate aftermath:*

Hannah Ahlers ~ Heather Alvarado ~ Dorene Anderson
Carrie Barnette ~ Jack Beaton ~ Steve Berger ~ Candice Bowers
Denise Burditus ~ Sandy Casey ~ Andrea Castilla
Denise Cohen ~ Austin Davis ~ Thomas Day Jr.
Christiana Duarte ~ Stacee Etcheber ~ Brian Fraser
Keri Galvan ~ Dana Gardner ~ Angela Gomez
Rocio Guillen Rocha ~ Charleston Hartfield
Christopher Hazencomb ~ Jennifer Irvine ~ Nicol Kimura
Jessica Klymchuk ~ Carly Kreibaum ~ Rhonda LeRocque
Victor Link ~ Jordan McIldoon ~ Kelsey Meadows ~ Calla Medig
Sonny Melton ~ Patricia Mestas ~ Austin Meyer ~ Adrian Murfitt
Rachael Parker ~ Jenny Parks ~ Carrie Parsons ~ Lisa Patterson
John Phippen ~ Melissa Ramirez ~ Jordyn Rivera
Quinton Robbins ~ Cameron Robinson ~ Tara Roe
Lisa Romero-Muniz ~ Chris Roybal ~ Brett Schwanbeck
Bailey Schweitzer ~ Laura Shipp ~ Erick Silva ~ Susan Smith
Brennan Stewart ~ Derrick "Bo" Taylor ~ Neysa Tonks
Michelle Vo ~ Kurt Von Tillow ~ Bill Wolfe Jr.

The two individuals who died from their injuries in the years following:

Kimberly Gervais ~ Samanta Arjune

Contents

PART THREE. STRONGER TOGETHER

Preface

For all the individual and institutional responses to urgent requests for help that came in during and after the Route 91 Harvest Festival mass shooting on October 1, 2017, we who call Las Vegas home have felt gratitude and humility. This collection is a way to acknowledge that gift, to honor those we lost, and to support survivors and their loved ones. Having lived in Southern Nevada for more than fifty years, I have seen the area's population grow from 300,000 to 2.4 million residents. I could not help asking how *strong* is *Vegas Strong* after experiencing this tragedy? The contributions to this collection helped me answer that question authoritatively in the affirmative. Las Vegas was made stronger by this tragedy as a result of our collective responses. Not only compassion but material help has supported and continues to support those who survived, their loved ones, and the larger place we call home, Las Vegas.

Each contribution offers a story of healing. As Claytee D. White, founding director of University of Nevada, Las Vegas, University Libraries' Oral History Research Center, helped me understand, every oral history is a story, a narrative. That reflection holds true for this collection. Each of these contributions begins as a personal story. Each author launches their perspective from memories of that night and the aftermath of the shooting. Readers will note the great diversity of perspectives. These voices include survivors and bereaved family members, medical and counseling professionals, academics, law enforcement, and politicians. I thought it important to keep the expressive styles, the formatting of contributions, and the diversity of voices clear. With this inclusive approach, stories validate one another for historical accuracy.

The gratitude I feel toward contributors who have shared the greatest pain possible and who trusted this process cannot be fully expressed. I hope this collection honors their vulnerability and generosity with dignity and respect. To the community members who said *yes* in a heartbeat, I am also grateful. I feel, as does the University of Nevada Press team, that this collection can help individuals, families, and communities engaged in the never-ending process of healing. I want to particularly thank the late Margaret Dalrymple, acquisitions editor for the University of Nevada Press, who believed in this collection from the moment I suggested it to her in early 2021. Also special thanks to Joanne Goodwin and Michael Green for help with the manuscript. To the communities who have faced or will be facing the terrible reality of hate and terrorism to respond at both the individual and communal level, we hope this collection helps.

Note: This book uses the term "1 October," which the public adopted as the reference to the tragic event that ended sixty lives as of this printing and irrevocably altered the lives of tens of thousands more. We use "October 1, 2017," when we refer to the date on which the event happened. The phrase "Vegas Strong" is an organic phrase, appearing the morning after the tragedy, and has come into common use.

VEGAS STRONG

Introduction

On October 10, 2017, Deryk Engelland, Vegas Golden Knights defenseman and for years a Las Vegas resident, spoke from the ice of T-Mobile Arena, ready for the first home game of the National Hockey League's newest team: "To the families and friends of the victims, know that we will do everything we can to help you and our city heal. We are Vegas Strong." First responders from 1 October led each member of the Golden Knights to the rink before the team faced off against the Arizona Coyotes. The team honored the victims of the massacre with 58 seconds of silence and would retire their jersey number 58. The team went on to do fundraisers, public announcements, to persist in raising awareness, and to forever be identified as a role model for community responsiveness. Like Engelland and the rest of the Golden Knights franchise, we of this collection seek to honor the victims and their families and friends with memory, compassion, and community.

Las Vegas had never experienced a mass shooting until the Route 91 Harvest Music Festival on October 1, 2017, when fifty-eight people were shot to death, with two more dying later of injuries. It was an event that wounded almost nine hundred other known victims physically and untold victims psychologically. The event on the Las Vegas Strip was the deadliest mass shooting to date in modern American history. Mass shootings continue to haunt the US at an alarming rate. They always seem to occur when victims are at their most vulnerable, with family and friends, praying, in the classroom, celebrating life.

During and after the tragedy, Las Vegas reinvented itself, as Steve Sisolak (then chair of the Clark County Commission and now governor of Nevada) expressed in *Healing Las Vegas: The Las Vegas Community Healing Garden in Response to the 1 October Tragedy*:

> I'll never forget driving down to the scene of one of the most horrific mass shootings in our nation's history the night of October 1, 2017. I clearly remember the sound of hundreds of cell phones, abandoned by their owners, ringing from loved ones checking in. That night exposed the darkest side of humanity and brought tragedy on fifty-eight families. It also brought out the best in our community—the community of Las Vegas—with countless people standing in line for hours to donate

blood, giving millions of dollars to the victims' fund, and building the beautiful Las Vegas Community Healing Garden to remember the victims and provide space for the community to heal. I've never been more proud of the Las Vegas community for coming together in a tremendous show of strength, unity, and love in one of the darkest times Las Vegas has seen, and in the years of hope and healing since.[1]

The voices of those who lived through the first moments and hours of this tragedy cry out in this collection and bring us back to those moments in their immediacy, heart-wrenching reality, and urgency.

In the section titled *Site,* we learn about the experience when the gunshots began from those who survived and from those of the community attending to victims and their loved ones in the immediate aftermath. The *Process* section includes voices of bereaved family members, community support, and reflections on bereavement, and we learn about the process of managing trauma and grief. The section *Stronger Together* includes ongoing institutionalized efforts to support, remember, and protect our community of survivors and our community at large.

Included in the *Site* section, recent University of Nevada, Las Vegas, graduate Ashley Primack explains how she escaped the bloodbath and how echoes of that night continue. Oral historian Barbara Tabach uses the words of festivalgoers and a professional photographer to help us understand the experience of being there and the impact on those who served that night, including a Las Vegas Metro Police officer, and the emergency doctors from the University Medical Center Level 1 trauma intensive care unit. Alicia (AC) Monrroy, UNLV Housing and Residential Life coordinator at the Dayton Complex, recalls the arrival of survivors fleeing the festival site about two and a half miles away. Roberta Sabbath, UNLV religious studies coordinator and Department of English visiting assistant professor, and with the help of Thomas Padilla, UNLV Lied Library digital specialist, interpret the almost one million tweets that those lost and wounded shared with their friends and families. Las Vegas mayor Carolyn Goodman explains her personal and her professional response to follow Federal Emergency Management Agency protocols and to help create the Las Vegas Community Healing Garden.

In the *Process* section, Mynda Smith, who lost her beloved sister, Neysa Christine Davis Tonks, takes us through the twenty-two-hour process after learning of Neysa's death. Claytee D. White, founding director of the Oral History Research Center at UNLV Libraries, enlists the journeys of three men: a survivor; a member of the Las Vegas Red Cross; and a protector of the tragedy's mementos and artifacts. Terri Keener, the Vegas Strong Resiliency Center's behavioral health coordinator, explains the traditional and innovative therapies that the center provides to 1 October survivors and their loved ones as well as cutting-edge collaborations with similarly devastated communities around the country. Laurie Lytel, professional social worker and volunteer therapist with the Vegas Strong Resiliency Center, explains the process of managing trauma. Daniel Bubb, an associate professor in residence at the UNLV Honors College, discusses the stages of mourning. Poet Eryn Green, a UNLV Department of English faculty member, reflects on the failure of words to express the pain of loss; he offers *"58 Bells"* and poems commemorating subsequent deaths as a result of the tragedy.

In the *Stronger Together* section, Tennille Pereira, director of the Vegas Strong Resiliency Center and chair of the 1 October Memorial Committee, explains the organic and determined development of this community bulwark to meet the legal, financial, and emotional needs of victims and their supporting friends and family. In addition, as Chairman of the 1 October Memorial Committee, Pereira discusses the process of preparing a proposal for the Clark County Commissioners for a permanent memorial commemorating the event and its victims. Stefani Evans, UNLV Libraries' oral historian and co-editor of *Healing Las Vegas: The Las Vegas Community Healing Garden in Response to the 1 October Tragedy,* documents how the garden was created in four days. The Clark County Museum's Cynthia Sanford, who has supervised the curation of more than twenty-two thousand artifacts stemming from the tragedy, explains how safeguarding these mementos is crucial for survivors and their loved ones. Congresswoman Dina Titus reports how her office responded with emergency assistance for survivors that included financial, investigative, and bureaucratic efforts. She continues to work toward a federal ban on bump stocks, a device that enables a semiautomatic rifle to fire faster, which was used in the shooting.

The work to fight hate continues. The need to heal never stops as a city never sleeps.

NOTES

1. Governor Steve Sisolak (then chair, Clark County Commission), in *Healing Las Vegas: The Las Vegas Community Healing Garden in Response to the 1 October Tragedy,* edited by Stefani Evans and Donna McAleer (Reno: University of Nevada Press, 2019), 95.

Part One

SITE

One October represents a day of unthinkable tragedy, terror, and loss. It also demonstrates the importance of collaboration, innovative training, and preparation for all first responders. Sometimes there is just pure evil in the world, and to combat that we must be united as one, committed to vigilance, engagement, and to staying resilient.

—SASHA LARKIN, Captain, Las Vegas Metropolitan Police Department, incident commander at the Route 91 Harvest Festival lot

It was humbling to speak to family members who lost loved ones. They were so grateful for our efforts to provide comfort, food, water, even if they couldn't eat or drink anything, at a location where we were trying to meet needs. It can be frustrating that you can't do enough, but all of us responded as we could, and it was enough. We stepped up. We came together as a community and supported the victims, the survivors with all we had. No one is completely over this. The event changed lives. There is no closure, really.

—JIM GIBSON, Clark County Commissioner

1

The Night That Forever Changed My Life

A Survivor's Story

Ashley Primack

In October 2017, my mom surprised me with VIP tickets to the Route 91 Harvest Music Festival. I grew up listening to country music with my family, and I was thrilled to be able to go to my first country music festival with the person who gave me my love for the genre. When we got there, I was euphoric. I will never forget the rush when I was surrounded by thousands of people who shared the same love for country music. We found our seats, and my mom and I danced and sang along to every artist as if nobody were watching us. Sam Hunt was headlining that night, and I was given the opportunity to go backstage while he was performing. There I met the singers who were overplayed on my playlists. I had to act as though I were not starstruck, but inside I thought the world was made of rainbows and butterflies. It is not every day that Maren Morris and Lauren Alaina sit at the same table as you while you watch the sweat drip off of Hunt. I was mesmerized, and I could not wait to see what the third day had in store.

The next day, Sunday, my mom told me she was not interested in going, but she said I could give the extra ticket to one of my friends. Since I had just turned seventeen, I was shocked that my mother would let me go to the Strip without her. After all of my girlfriends declined on the last-minute offer, I invited my closest boyfriend. He and I had dated a few times, so I knew he would be over the moon to go to this festival. With only a few hours of notice, he did not hesitate to say yes. I felt like such an adult because the only times I had ever been to the Strip was with my parents. I picked him up on my own and off we went! We went to our

VIP booth and sang and danced all night. Our seats were stage left, closest to Mandalay Bay. Even though we were the youngest people in our booth, we quickly became friends with the adults near us, dancing and singing along to every lyric.

There were only two more sets by Big & Rich and Jake Owen before Jason Aldean would close the festival. Aldean was one of my first introductions to country. "Hicktown" and "Amarillo Sky" came out when I was only five years old. At this time in my life, his album *They Don't Know* was released, and I was prepared for every lyric on that album. The crowd went crazy when Big & Rich performed their new "California." I will also never forget how the energy of the crowd built as Owen performed. Everyone was screaming Owen's lyrics of "Barefoot Blue Jean Night." Once that set ended, we knew what was next, and I could feel the screaming from the crowd in my chest. We were just overwhelmed with excitement.

Now it was time for Aldean. He stepped on stage, and it was one of the best feelings to see him in person. He sounded just like he did on his albums. When he sang "When She Says Baby," there were sporadic sounds that reminded me of fireworks. We thought that was strange because it would only make sense for the festival to blast off fireworks to close the three-day festival, rather than in the middle of a song. We were all distracted by the noise, and everyone looked around trying to spot the fireworks. Time passed, Aldean continued to perform, but the mood in the crowd changed. The noise was still sporadically blasting, and the people near us were trying to convince us that it was not a gun. How could it be? We went through metal detectors, and surely a semi-automatic rifle would set off the machine. I had also never heard a real gunshot in my life. Aldean was still performing. As long as he did not think anything was wrong, why should we? Some people thought the unexpected outbursts could have been the sound of his speaker being blown out. This was also believable. Still in our VIP section, we all convinced ourselves that nothing was wrong. Seeing nothing, we tried to not let the sound ruin our experience of watching one of the biggest country performers sing. The volume of the crowd shouting the lyrics slowly began to die down. A few moments later, in the middle of his song, we saw Aldean run off of the stage. Now we knew something was really wrong. The periods of time in between the blasts were getting shorter and shorter, and I knew our intuition was correct.

The first thing I did was call my mom. I said, "Mom, there is a shooter at the concert." At the time, she said she thought I meant one person was shot. She did not think her baby girl was going to be a victim of a mass shooting. Why would she think that? This kind of event is something you would only hear on the news, not something that actually happens to you. It was not until she could hear the gunshots echo through the phone when her calmness switched to panic. Her daughter, who was in a severe car accident just seven days before, was in what would turn into the largest mass shooting in modern US history. Flustered, she handed the phone to my stepdad. They bolted out of bed and headed straight to us. We lived about twenty-five minutes away, so he told me to shout out everything I saw, including text on the signs that I saw.

Escaping the venue seemed almost impossible. People were running in every direction trying to find a way out. My stepdad directed me to find another exit that was not flooded with people. He said a shooter will typically aim in the direction with groups of people rather than at relatively isolated singles or couples. As we searched for places to go, we watched people getting hit by bullets in all directions, and the length of the breaks in between the blasts was unpredictable. We could not hide in the same spot for too long. There was no safe area to be. We thought the shooter (or shooters) was on the ground with us, so we ran as fast as we could every chance we got. During the shooting periods, my friend pushed me down, laying on top of me, to protect me from a potential wound. We saw people screaming, crying, and searching for their loved ones with whom they had entered the festival. As we were running, we saw people taking off their cowboy boots, dropping their purses, and leaving the rest of their belongings. During one of the blasting periods, I was pushed down next to someone who was unconscious and bleeding. To this day, I have no idea who they were or if they made it to tell their story. Still on the phone, my stepdad was able to hear every time I was body slammed on the asphalt, but I made sure to stay on the phone. I wanted them to hear my voice. Staying silent would only provoke even more panic in my parents.

Once we finally escaped the venue, we headed straight for the Tropicana hotel-casino just north of the concert venue. Since we were so far from the exit, it took us much longer to escape. By this point, many in the crowd had already taken cover here, and every door was locked. We were sprinting up an escalator to search for any room to take cover, but with all of my adrenaline, I slipped, falling down several steps. I had no time to react to the pain that my body had already endured throughout the night, and I kept running. Eventually, we found a young couple in their early twenties, dressed in country gear, headed for the service elevator. With nothing to lose, we asked if we could join them. They welcomed us with open arms, stating they had a room in the hotel, and we could stay with them until my parents came to get us. I told my parents the room number, but I wanted to hang up to call my father. He had no idea I was at the festival. I told him everything I had just witnessed, and he broke down. My strong father, the man who never cried, the man to whom I looked up, was speechless about what I had endured. He wanted me to keep him updated, but my phone was almost out of battery power. I wanted to conserve as much power as possible to be sure my mom could find me in the hotel.

We turned on the news, and stations were reporting a rumor that there was another active shooter in the Tropicana. Where I thought I had found safety, I immediately was flooded with tears. I did not think I was going to make it out to safety. In that very moment, the twentysomething man in the room pulled out a gun without any explanation. I initially thought he was the man who was rumored to be the shooter. As he watched the tears dropping onto my shirt, he comforted me, showing me his Los Angeles Police Department badge. He wanted to us to know that he would protect us for as long as we were in his room. The amount of relief I felt was unexplainable.

Moments later, my parents knocked on the room door. I could barely stand when I felt my mom wrap her arms around me. I had never been so grateful to have her with me in my entire life. We thanked the young couple for helping us and wished them the best of luck for the night. I asked my parents how long it took to come rescue us, and my mom said it was only about thirty-five minutes since I initially called her about the gunshots. As we left the property, we had to exit down the escalator. Silence filled the lobby, and we thought we were alone and safe. A wall blocked our vision, however, and we suddenly heard a man's deep voice yelling, "Put your hands up." For some reason, the yelling triggered something in me, and my eyes flooded with tears once again. He perhaps thought we were the perpetrators. He was a member of the SWAT team, and he directed us to exit through the employee tunnel in the Tropicana. In the tunnel were hundreds of people, covered in blood, waiting to be seen by paramedics. Most of them were separated from their concert companions.

Once we finally got into the car, I remember the silence that filled it. My friend and I could not speak about what we had just seen. It felt like we were running for safety for what seemed like hours. We saw several pickup trucks with injured passengers in the bed transporting them to hospitals. We dropped my friend off at his home. I called my dad, letting him know that I would be home soon. He expressed how sorry he was that I had to go through this. I asked my mom how she got to us so quickly. She said no police officers blocked the roads at the time. I was so lucky that I called them when I did because otherwise they might not have been able to get to us.

When we got home, I went straight to my bathroom. I wanted to be alone for a minute. When I walked into the lit-up bathroom, I looked at myself in the mirror, and I was shocked at my appearance. This was the first time I had taken the time to see myself. I looked down to see blood soaked into my white Converse shoes. There was blood on the ends of my flannel shirt, which I had tied around my waist. My knees, elbows, and palms were stained with black from the asphalt. My mascara had dripped down my cheeks. I cleaned myself off, and the first thing I did after that was crawl into bed with my mom. I was still in complete shock, and although I was home, I did not feel safe for some reason. The world that I had trusted to be filled with good people had a completely different image for me. I was afraid of someone coming to my house to hurt me or my family. All I wanted to do was stay in my mom's room and never leave.

The next day was a Monday. I woke up feeling incredibly sore from all my bruises. I had no more adrenaline to mask the injuries I had endured the night before. I had broken two ribs. To this day, I will never know if that was from the first or successive body slams or from my slip on the escalator. Although I was supposed to be at school, I could not bear to leave my house. I was not able to sleep through the night, and most of all, I was petrified. I received what seemed like hundreds of calls and texts to make sure I was okay. I even received a text from one of my teachers. I was numb in each response. I only wanted to talk to my friend who had been at the concert with me. He came over to visit me that night, but I was in no way okay. I was hurting. I was hurting for the people who did not make it out that night. I was hurting for the families of the deceased. I was hurting for the wounded. Selfishly, I was hurting for myself.

The next day, I decided to go to school. My parents thought I should leave the house and have some social interactions. Locking myself in my house would not do any good for my mental health. I was just going through the motions in each of my classes. The only thing getting me through my day was practice for my dance team. After dance practice that day, my coach pulled me aside and asked if I would feel comfortable changing our routine to a remembrance piece of 1 October. Without hesitation, I said yes. Our Vegas Strong performance placed tenth in a national competition.

Although I was able to start living my life like I used to, I still struggle in many ways. After that night, I brought an inflatable mattress into my mom's room, and I slept in there for weeks until I felt safe. I would have flashbacks of my experience when I would hear any loud noises. Loud electronic dance music, sirens, the school bell, and yelling would all take me back to that terrible night. I've dreaded the Fourth of July since the attack. Although I have traditionally spent this joyous holiday with friends, I began reliving the scene of that night with each blast of fireworks. To this day, I am constantly aware of emergency exits when I enter a new place, especially with large amounts of people. I went to The Smith Center downtown to watch a musical with my dad that December, and all I could do was stare at the exit. While these symptoms of post-traumatic stress disorder are fading as the years progress, I recently realized that there is one trigger that has not gotten easier. This year, my mother took me to a Toby Keith concert. While we were waiting for the show to start, country music played on the speakers. When Jason Aldean's "When She Says Baby," came on, I broke down. I can still hear the shots behind the music when this song plays. I am still working through symptoms like these.

October 1 will never be the same for me. I still talk to the boy who went to the festival with me on that date every year. Although I left Las Vegas to attend college, my old teachers, friends, and family remember to check in with me on that day to make sure I am okay. I am extremely grateful for the support system that I have had along the way. While I am thankful that I left that night without severe injuries, I would not wish this experience on anyone.

The Las Vegas community has grown to become closer since this tragedy. From now until forever, we will be Vegas Stronger.

2

The Night the Music Stopped

Snapshots from Oral Histories

Barbara Tabach, Oral Historian,
Oral History Research Center, UNLV Libraries

On October 1, 2017, time rushed at us like a tidal wave and cruelly scarred the date forever into history. How could our community, any community, absorb the shock and trauma of a mass casualty event? Were our friends safe and well? Was there something each of us could do to be of help? What. Could. We. Do. What had happened to us all?

Unquestionably, there is a great measure of truth that only a survivor of a tragedy can fully know, and understand, their experience. As a local oral historian, my objective in listening to others is to collect, preserve, and archive the firsthand accounts of events and people in Las Vegas's history. In the months following October, I would become a collector of the personal stories of the Route 91 Harvest Festival tragedy.

Within the *telling* of the oral histories, the *seeing* crystalizes. Considering the brutal enormity of the shooting—the thousands who fled the festival grounds, the hundreds of wounded who managed to survive, the dozens who perished, and the first responders who would have their own memories to share—one can imagine but not fully know what transpired. It is a cherished honor to have been asked by the Oral History Research Center at UNLV Libraries to listen to and record the memories of those intimately touched by this heartbreak.

The following excerpts memorialize the scene where innocent country music fans became targets of a deranged shooter. The whirlwind of chaos spilled twenty-two thousand festivalgoers into the streets, not knowing what was transpiring or where to seek refuge. Among them, hundreds of injured were shuttled to hospitals in the back of strangers' trucks or by passing Ubers or cab drivers just wanting to help.

To this day, the shooter's motivation is not understood. And, to this day, the aching grief it caused permeates the Las Vegas community from the doctor who slipped out of the hospital to snap a photo of the sun rising to remind him it was a new day to the police officer who tearfully hugged his wife and children the next day to the Red Cross volunteer who provided kindness in the search for understanding.

The almost seventy oral histories collected for the Remembering 1 October project are archived in Special Collections and Archives at UNLV's Lied Library. They are honest and direct accounts from a cross section of festival attendees, first responders, medical personnel, therapists, and others who pulled together in the aftermath. They are first-hand documentation of experiences and observations shared without adornment.

These narrative snapshots illustrate how the festival scene rapidly expands beyond the distance between the shooter, who is cowardly poised in his hotel room window across the street, and his target of country music fans enjoying the Route 91 Harvest Festival. Abruptly, the site erupts in the time after 10:04 p.m. into a horror that will remain a part of each of us who live in and love Las Vegas.

10 p.m. ~ October 1

On the night of Sunday, October 1, 2017, my husband and I are at a friend's house sipping wine and enjoying a soft autumn breeze while gazing at the Strip in the distance. Random clouds skirt across the Las Vegas skyline. It is a beautiful evening. Among the topics we discuss is that tonight is also the Vegas Golden Knights' final exhibition game to prepare for their inaugural season. Las Vegas is excited and proud to have a major league sports team.

By ten o'clock, most hockey fans have either returned home or are still partying on the Strip. At this hour, the annual Route 91 Harvest Festival has welcomed Jason Aldean to the main stage. Las Vegas is alive and doing what it does best.

It is the last act of the third and final day of the music festival. Backstage, Dave Becker, a professional photographer, is editing images of Aldean that he took a few minutes before. Becker is on assignment with Getty Images and has covered the music festival since its inception in 2014. He says: "Over the years, I've done annual events that keep coming back here (to Las Vegas). I think it was 2014, the first event that I photographed of the Route 91 Festival. . . . It's a three-day event. It's long days. They're fun. Up until about ten o'clock that night, it was the same as it's always been. I photographed dozens of performers over three days, a lot of entertainment, a lot of food, a lot of drinking, a lot of fans."[1]

It's also been a busy day at University Medical Center's emergency room. At ten o'clock, the day-shift doctors are still on duty, well past their usual end time of 7 p.m. Under the leadership of Dr. Deborah Kuhls, they are finalizing the transfer of patients to her night-shift partner, Dr. Syed Saquib. He recalls in his oral history: "There were still a lot of loose ends from the daytime that we needed to tie up, so they were still around. I and my resident team were there from 7 p.m. onward."[2]

10:05 P.M. ~ OCTOBER 1

Back at the festival, at exactly 10:04 p.m., Danielle McLaughlin snaps a happy selfie of herself and her husband near the main stage. They have attended each Route 91 concert and are avid fans of Aldean. This is a staycation weekend for them; they are staying across the street at Mandalay Bay.

Abruptly, a staccato of popping rat-ta-tat sounds punctures the music of Aldean singing his hit song "When She Says Baby." Suddenly the music is halted. McLaughlin recalls: "Everyone had said it sounded like fireworks, and it really, truly did sound like fireworks."[3]

But it wasn't. Within seconds, the McLaughlins and their friends find themselves in the thicket of chaos. Their bewilderment turns to adrenaline-infused determination to escape the festival grounds as they notice that one of their group members has been shot in his leg. He is still able to run.

Throngs begin rushing frantically, trusting the wisdom of attendees confident of the direction of the shots. As more bullets riddle the crowd, the crush of attendees is now rushing to whatever exit they can locate. In those sixty seconds from the taking of a selfie at 10:04 to the first shots at 10:05, the party spirit vanishes. Lives are being forever transformed. The horror is spontaneously unfolding.

Of those minutes, Becker recalls his startled curiosity about the popping noises. Backstage, everyone around him seems to momentarily accept the fireworks explanation or that it was a malfunction of sound equipment. He continues: "I went back to work editing the last performer, who was Jason Aldean. A few moments later, people started streaming by the little entryway to the tent—the fans, the crowd was streaming through. . . . As the audience starts passing through and I make a phone call to my colleague to find out if he had heard anything, he hadn't heard, but he would look into it. It turns out he had just got home from photographing one of the Knights hockey games that was the same night."[4]

Another festival attendee, Andrea Gardea, describes getting separated from her brother and his wife as the shots rang out:

> My brother and his wife were together. But somehow I alone ended up underneath a bar table by myself not knowing where anybody was at. At that point, I lost everyone. All I remember once I realized I was under a bar table is turning around looking at some guy who is holding me down, just saying, "Stay down." I don't know who he is. He just has these eyes, and I can see fear in his eyes. I can see him heavy breathing. In slow motion almost, I feel like, is this really happening? And I'm like, oh my gosh. Then it hits me that this is really happening. As I turn around, I see one girl just down. She gets shot as she's running out and just face down. At that point, I'm like, how is this going to happen? Is this real? Is this seriously real? We were there for a couple of rounds, and then I remember just hearing the guy say, "Okay, run . . ."[5]

In the midst of the frantic moments, Becker instinctively grabs his camera and maneuvers his way out of the tent. He explains: "It was difficult because by then much of the crowd is filtering through this narrow area where I can exit to the audience area. So it would be difficult for me to get through there because I would be like a salmon going upstream. It would be literally impossible without being knocked down or blocking the way."[6]

Undaunted, Becker manages to make his way through the fencing and steps up on a table hoping to get a better view of the scene:

> It was about a six-foot high fence with a fabric shield, so you couldn't really see through it. I looked down once I got on the table and I can see the people are panicking and running in all directions. I focused mostly on the people coming right at me. That's when I started to photograph the people. . . .
>
> It was a few minutes later when the crowd eventually thinned out where I was able to get down off the table and make my way into the

concert grounds. I didn't go very far. Again, in the back of my mind, I'm thinking, it's only the speakers that are popping. Why are all these people running? Honestly, I am thinking to myself, they're just running out of the abundance of caution or they're panicking because they think the worst.

I didn't see at that moment anything that would tell me that there was an actual shooter other than the repeated sounds of the popping, which I heard, as everybody else has heard, over and over again for the ten minutes.

It was dark. A lot of the lights had gone out, so there was one light here and lights in the background. I did what I could to make solid images knowing that whatever it is, it's going to be important. I can't say for sure that I knew what was going on. Again, I kept telling myself it was only the speakers that were popping. Over the course of the months since the event, I've thought about it over and over again, and I've heard those popping sounds over and over again that maybe I didn't want to believe anything was bad.

I saw people lying on the ground; I photographed them. I thought perhaps they're just sort of playing possum; they were just lying still for fear; they couldn't move; they didn't want to move. People were running by me. One woman tripped next to me as she was trying to jump over some fencing. She didn't have any shoes on. Other people were streaming by me in front of the vending booths. People crying. . . .

It was journalistic instinct for me to grab my cameras and photograph. Whatever it was going on, something was going on. Whether it was something as tragic as it happened or it was just a panic because the speakers were blasting, when [members of] the crowd are exiting in such mass amounts, someone is going to get hurt, someone is going to get trampled. Someone can get physically hurt or even possibly die because of a mass panic, and that's what was growing through my mind as to what was going on, and that's why the journalist in me kicked in and said, "This is going to be news, whatever it is." It could last a day, the news; nobody was physically hurt. But during a concert, people are exiting the arena in crazy hysteria.[7]

Within moments after 10:05, first responders are learning of a mass attack occurring at the Route 91 Harvest Festival. The UMC's Trauma

Intensive Care Unit receives a call alerting Kuhls, lead trauma physician, to prepare for about fifty to one hundred shooting injuries. She explains:

> We were almost finished with the disposition of our daytime patients. I was on call with residents, and we were as a team still there. . . . There were actually two trauma surgery teams on call.
>
> We work in an area that's a little different than most hospitals. UMC has a hospital-within-a hospital concept, so we have an emergency room, operating rooms, CAT scan, angio suite where we can some-times stop bleeding without an operation, and a fourteen-bed trauma intensive care unit that are in kind of a separate but connected build-ing. In addition to that we have a main emergency department that is located several hundred yards away that is for adults. We have a pedi-atric emergency room, as well, that's in the same building as the trauma center but on the third floor. That's kind of important as we talk about 1 October because within the trauma center we really focus on trauma, and gunshot wounds would be some of the high acute traumas that we would see. So we're staffed by the team that I described, plus there's a full-time emergency medic attending and that person may or may not have a resident working with them. That's the staff that was there.[8]

Her partner, Saquib, recalls that he was "initially in a state of shock because I didn't want to believe it. I thought it might have been a false alarm or some hoax. But then once they verified that this is legitimate, then I realized, okay, we need to spring into action."[9]

Any tiredness that Kuhls and her team felt quickly dissipates. The UMC emergency physicians set up a triage area outside the hospital building. In her oral history, she describes the sequence of events within the hospital, assessing the injuries, and working with the medical person-nel that grows to include Dr. John Fildes (the director of UMC trauma), military surgeons, nurses, respiratory therapists, administrators, ICU staff, and those who transported the injured to the hospital. She details steps taken, from identifying patients to updating the media.

As all the hospitals in Las Vegas go on alert, the twenty-two thou-sand dazed people are dispersing into the streets; into nearby hotels; to the Thomas & Mack Center parking lot on the campus of the University of Nevada, Las Vegas; to the nearby Shrine of the Most Holy Redeemer Roman Catholic church, to the grounds of McCarran (now Harry Reid)

International Airport. Wherever their unknowing energies might carry them. Hundreds suddenly realize they are wounded and in need of assistance.

One shooting victim, Christina Gruber, describes becoming separated from her friends: "[I] ended up at the church down the street where I had realized I had been hit while I was running. I looked down. It was just like a popping feeling. I looked down at my legs and saw blood coming down and that kind of prompted me to run faster. Through my head that entire time, I was just wanting to get home to my kids."

At the church, a couple from California performed triage on her:

[The husband] used the belt off of his pants and created a tourniquet on my leg. . . . [Then he] piggybacked me to the main street where I got into a stranger's car with other victims. I remember there was a man in the front seat; his name was Bruce, and he had been shot in the foot. I was at that point just panicking. He just held my hand and tried to keep me calm.

Meanwhile, [the couple] from California, they had my phone and one of my boots; they had taken my boot off in order to get the tourniquet on my leg, so I didn't have my phone at the hospital. But she was taking phone calls from everybody calling from all over the country, letting them know I had been hit and that I was on my way to the hospital.[10]

Gruber would be transferred to another hospital where her life and her leg were saved. A bullet had dangerously pierced her thigh. Of her immediate days of recuperation, she says: "From October to December, I barely knew what day it was. I woke up, and I just went through the motions of getting up, going to work, trying to perform my job. I don't think I was even thinking clearly enough to perform my job. I was just still in this cloud of, What just happened here? Did it really happen?"[11]

AFTER 11:00 P.M. ~ OCTOBER 1

Earlier in the evening, Steve Riback, Las Vegas Metro Police sergeant, had been working an overtime assignment for the Golden Knights crowd at T-Mobile Arena. He had just slipped into bed when the alerts of an active shooter at Mandalay Bay roused him. He recalls:

I could hear panic and desperation, confusion. I mean, the whole gamut of emotions were running through my head.

It was probably shortly after eleven at that point, and I was absolutely confused of what was going on. I was like, wow. I just wasn't processing of like, wow, this is really happening. At one point, I glanced at my clock on the car radio and I saw that it was just shortly after eleven. I'm like, oh, wow, it's not the middle of night. I had only been asleep maybe a half-hour or forty-five minutes at that point.

So I could hear active shooter. I heard Mandalay Bay. I heard MGM [Grand], New York-New York, Paris, Bellagio; all these hotels were having reports. The dispatcher was reporting, saying, citizens are hearing gunshots at this location or that location, or they're seeing somebody with rifles enter/exit the hotel. Officers were getting on saying they're hearing reports of active shooters at this hotel. It was just absolute chaos. I was just like, wow, this is just . . . It was insane, for lack of a better word. I couldn't believe that it was happening. I would never say anything like, wow, I never thought that would happen here, because it's just not the case. For me, it's not an "if it's going to ever happen," it's "when and to what degree."[12]

Riback describes flying down Interstate 215 to his station off the Cheyenne Avenue exit and seeing police cars racing with lights and sirens toward the Strip. The protocol was to meet up with his squad at their station, and from there they went to Spring Valley Hospital. "We got there, and it was very surreal. . . . There were doctors and nurses and medical staff everywhere; I mean, there were bodies and people everywhere. I saw gurneys of people lined down the hall. I could see as soon as you walked in they were doing some sort of medical intervention to somebody over to the left."

As he continued into the emergency room, he saw patients being triaged:

Some were still coming in. . . . We had heard on the radio different people were being transported by different methods. People were literally being thrown into backs of pickup trucks or were on the side of the road and somebody picked them up and dropped them off.

Through the remainder of the night, into the morning, we were tasked with interviewing and identifying the victims from the incident. . . . We had well over forty victims. We had several deaths that were there. We just methodically went down through lists; every hour or two, we would check with medical to get updated lists to make sure we were dealing with the right people, the people that were there that were supposed to be there in terms of did they need to go to other facilities.[13]

The news of a fellow officer's death during the shooting ripples through first responders. Charles Hartfield, an off-duty Las Vegas Metro Police officer, was among the fifty-eight killed that night at the site. Riback returns home hours later to the warming hugs of his wife and three school-aged children. Tearfully he recalls:

I lost it because I was like, man . . . Twenty years in law enforcement, I've been through crazy situations where I'm like, my God, thank you, I'm still alive, and I know a lot of cops deal with that. There's also several cops on my department who have never come home from situations. I was so thankful, so grateful. My kids had seen me when I walked in, and I gave my wife a hug. My oldest had said, "Abba"— father, dad—"Why are you crying?" I just hugged my kids. We sat them down, and I just said to them, "There was a bad person who hurt a lot of people." It was tough. That was one of the hardest things I remember as a parent, as a parent/police officer telling my kids that something had happened.[14]

Entering the Festival Grounds
In time, investigators were allowed into the festival grounds. Clark County coroner John Fudenberg remembers entering the festival grounds after eleven o'clock to what he describes as "a wave of red Solo® cups that were going back and forth because they were captured with the wind, literally a wave of them hitting from your knee down."[15]

For many responders, it is the sea of cell phones going off that is forever etched into memory. Charles L. Hank III, a Las Vegas Metro Police officer, talks about his decision to walk across Las Vegas Boulevard from Mandalay Bay to the festival grounds. He shares: "SWAT is clearing the hotel. I just was there managing that at the hotel. . . . [I] went with another captain over to the venue. . . . [I] walked across the street, which I wish I hadn't done. To hear those cell phones ringing and nobody answering—that's pretty heavy on my mind, those people calling their folks. And then they stopped for a while, and when the morning came they started ringing again. You know someone is looking for their loved one."[16]

3 P.M. ~ OCTOBER 2

The hours ticked away into a strange eeriness. Las Vegas locals and tourists are all immersed in this massive community trauma. Each person wants, needs, to help. To demonstrate in some way how we are all in this together. People donate blood, deliver food to first responders, set up help centers and memorials.

When Kuhls talks about driving home about three that next afternoon, her eyes well up with tears. She drives west on Charleston Boulevard, away from the hospital where she has been since seven in the morning of October 1. Ahead she sees:

> All kinds of police . . . redirecting traffic, and then we have those signs that lanes were closing. I thought I was coming up onto a motor vehicle crash. There were literally thousands of people at the main blood donation [center], so much so that they were actually stepping out into the street, and we didn't want to hit them. . . . I wish I had had a camera, because I'm just like, wow, this is just overwhelming, the number of people. . . . I really thought it was a motor vehicle crash. Then I saw the blood donation at Delta Point. I really knew that the community was activated, but it almost seemed like ten times the effect at the main blood donation center. I'm like, this is really impressive for our city or any city.[17]

When she arrives home, almost one hundred emails and text messages await her. Concerned professionals offering assistance, making sure she is okay. As she attempts to answer them, sleep takes the upper hand, and she drifts off until sometime the next day.

When Saquib is asked if this tragedy has tainted his image of Las Vegas, he responds:

> No, no, no. If anything, it's given me even a more positive view of Las Vegas because people banded together so well, from the first responders to all the good Samaritans at that concert that were helping each other out, whether it was trying to rush people to safety or using their

belts as tourniquets to stop hemorrhage or those Uber drivers or taxi drivers who were taking patients by the manyfold in their cars and rushing them to hospitals. The community response was great not just in the moment but afterward as well. We kind of showed the world that we're not just a tourist city. We have two million people here that are part of this community that love this city. We are, as we have said multiple times, Vegas Strong. I'm not going to let this one guy, whose name I don't even want to know and try not to remember, this one guy who created so much carnage define us. I'm going to look at the stuff that happened afterward to define our city.[18]

Feeling Purpose

The oral histories became my way to feel purpose in the aftermath of the tragedy.

So here we are five years later. Like magnets, the oral histories that we have collected grip to each other to create one story of our community in the aftermath of the largest mass casualty event in recent history. The tragedy enveloped the entire city, from the festival grounds to the hospitals, from the trauma intervention center to police stations. It included human stories of surviving, healing, helping, struggling. Stories of the preciousness of families and friends, and the hope within tomorrows.

The music abruptly stopped that night. And time was suspended. As each year passes, we bear witness to the fact that time is not a wave that washes away the trauma. The memories of a heinous arsenal of weapons remain with us as a ghostly reminder of the sadness, as well as a reminder of the kindnesses that heal.

I am grateful to those who participated in the Remembering 1 October Oral History Project. Your stories matter.

Notes

1. David Becker, an oral interview for Remembering 1 October Oral History Project, interview by Barbara Tabach and Claytee D. White, May 15, 2018, 3.

2. Dr. Syed Saquib, an oral interview for Remembering 1 October Oral History Project, interview by Barbara Tabach, February 22, 2018, 1.

3. Danielle McLaughlin, an oral interview for Remembering 1 October Oral History Project, interview by Barbara Tabach, February 14, 2018.

4. Becker, 3–5.

5. Andrea Gardea, an oral interview for Remembering 1 October Oral History Project, interview by Barbara Tabach, June 26, 2019, 8.

6. Becker, 5.

7. Becker, 6–7.

8. Dr. Deborah Kuhls, An Oral Interview for Remembering 1 October Oral History Project, Interview by Barbara Tabach, December 29, 2017, 2.

9. Saquib, 1.

10. Christina Gruber, An Oral Interview for Remembering 1 October Oral History Project, Interview by Barbara Tabach, March 2, 2019, 3–4.

11. Gruber, 11.

12. Sergeant Steve Riback, An Oral Interview for Remembering 1 October Oral History Project, Interview by Barbara Tabach, December 12, 2017, 3.

13. Riback, 4–5.

14. Riback, 7.

15. John Fudenberg, An Oral Interview for Remembering 1 October Oral History Project, Interview by Barbara Tabach and Claytee D. White, May 3, 2018, 7.

16. Charles Lee Hank III, An Oral Interview for Remembering 1 October Oral History Project, Interview by Claytee D. White and Barbara Tabach, April 10, 2019, 18.

17. Kuhls, 18–19.

18. Saquib, 12.

3

This Was Not in the Manual

UNLV *Residence Hall Becomes Safe Haven*

ALICIA (AC) MONRROY, UNLV Housing and Residential
Life Coordinator for Dayton Complex

I served as a Housing and Residential Life Coordinator for the Dayton
Complex residence hall at University of Nevada, Las Vegas, and I have
been a Residential Life staff member for seven years. The night of the
October 1, 2017, shooting, I was in my residence hall getting ready for
bed and preparing for the workweek when I received a text from my colleague and friend Eric Morrow about police activity at Mandalay Bay.
When I learned about the police activity occurring, I turned on the TV
and saw the news headline about a shooting at the Route 91 Harvest
Festival. Moments later, one of my resident assistants called me about
Dayton residents seeing individuals running toward them and appearing scared and frantic with blood on their clothes. The individuals shared
with staff that someone began shooting concert attendees at the festival, and they ran until they found people to help. They called University
Police Services, and Lisamarie Tomassetti, the coordinator on call, took
them to our residence hall conference room, where they could charge
their phones to call family members, talk to police about what happened,
and, most importantly, be in a safe space.

When I arrived to help the resident assistants, I went into a hallway
and found a distressed man on the phone. He appeared to be lost. When
I asked him if he was okay, he said he was bartending at the concert and
ran away when he heard the gunshots. He didn't know where he was, and
I took him to the conference room to meet with police. He was so scared
to go back outside, so in that moment, I knew I had to be confident in
assuring him I was here for him and would get him to safety.

When we arrived at the conference room, Tomassetti, my RA duty staff members Elle Cross and Anna Opara, and a police officer were with the victims who had fled the concert. Morrow arrived shortly after with bottled water and snacks, and we looked through boxes of old program T-shirts to give them so they didn't have to wear their bloody clothes. Another festivalgoer, Ryan (no last name given), arrived at Dayton and said his friends were somewhere near campus but were lost. We discovered through FaceTime that they had run all the way to the baseball fields. With the help of University Police Services, however, we were able to reunite them with Ryan at Dayton. When he was able to see his friends, they sobbed in each other's arms. It took everything in me to not go over to them and hug every single one of them while I held back my tears. One of the individuals ran so hard and far that her shoes fell off and the bottoms of her feet were black and dirty. I ran over to my apartment and grabbed a pair of socks and shoes to give her. Unfortunately, the shoes were too small for her. The socks were fine, and she was grateful to have something on her feet. We laughed when she commented on how tiny the shoes were compared to her feet, and it made us forget everything happening around us for a quick moment.

An hour or so went by before the victims were able to find rides to off-campus locations. All of the individuals except for the bartender were from out of state visiting for the music festival, so it took some time for them to find an opportunity to leave. We stayed in the room with them until their rides came and didn't leave their sides until we saw them ride away.

I felt helpless when I couldn't completely comfort the victims nor tell them everything was going to be okay because I knew this night was going to be with them forever. I kept asking how I could help them, and one woman told me, "Please don't leave us alone." I briefly felt relief and comfort when they were able to get rides off campus. They were so grateful for all of our help, though the entire time I felt like I wasn't doing enough for them. My UNLV Housing and Residential Life family members were truly my rocks that night and early morning, and I know I couldn't have gotten through it all without them. I am so lucky and grateful to work with amazing folks like them.

Whenever I think about that night and everything that happened in my building afterward, I feel incredibly sad and wonder what else we could have done for those victims. Anytime I talk about it with folks, it takes everything in me not to cry. I am fighting back tears while I write this story in my office and blaming allergies if any student asks if I'm okay. Luckily, when I need to talk with someone about it, I have a lot of great folks around me who are understanding and nonjudgmental when the tears flow.

I've been told many times that even though I wasn't at the concert and didn't experience the tragedy directly, I am still emotionally and mentally affected because of how I assisted the victims who fled to my residence hall. The shoes I offered to the young woman are still sitting in my office since the morning of October 2. I can't seem to find the strength to move them, take them home, or give them away.

4

Transforming Platforms

Greek Chorus and Social Media

ROBERTA SABBATH, visiting assistant professor, UNLV Department
of English; Director, UNLV Religious Studies Program

What I did not appreciate until making the connection between the
Greek chorus of Sophocles' tragedy *Oedipus Rex* and contemporary social
media is what hides in plain sight, the narrative of the chorus and social
media themselves. The chorus and social media speak for everyman, in
their essentially democratic form. What were those citizens of Athens
thinking, worrying about, and feeling during the plague and the Peloponnesian War in 430 BCE when *Oedipus Rex* appeared, and the citizens of Las Vegas during the 1 October bloodbath in 2017? How did they
express the need to stop the death and dying? How does a city survive
when one-third to two-thirds of its population succumbs to a deadly
blight and a war or experiences the worst mass shooting in modern US
history? In their moments of tragedy, citizens of Athens and Las Vegas
stood and stand united.

The theater has long been recognized as a liminal space that plays
out the sacred rites of passage and ritualizes dramatic change and crisis
management in the lives of individuals and communities. Victor Turner's description of change and crisis management mirrors the ideal plot
that Aristotle suggests in his *Poetics:* plot movement from status quo,
through disruption and conflict, to a reconfigured status quo. Turner's terms are helpful here. The narrative arc of the three Turner stages
expressed through the lines of the chorus and the tweets of social media
parallel the emotional trajectory in real time:

1. Separation—recognition of radical change in the status quo
2. Liminal period—period of transformation
3. Aggregation—reconstituted status quo[1]

Vocalized by a choral entity and social media, Turner's three-pronged stages here represent the performance of civic duty, the universal responsibility of citizenry to confront a catastrophic threat.

After explaining the historical contexts of ancient Athens and modern Las Vegas, I compare Turner's stages using lines of the chorus from the Greek play and social media metadata collected within seventy-two hours of the Las Vegas tragedy. While Sophocles' play written 2,500 years ago had its choral voices express citizen trauma, the almost one million hyperlinks and image tweets, captured as metadata by UNLV digital specialist Thomas Padilla, express the story of festivalgoers and citizens alike.[2] Both media—choral voices and social media—reflect a community plunged into shock and grief, asking who and why, and attempting to help their city.

When *Oedipus the King* first appeared, Athenian audiences needed a distraction. Athens faced two physical threats to its very existence, both the plague and the Peloponnesian War. They also questioned the wisdom of their leader, Pericles.[3]

According to David Wiles, around the time of the play, when Athens was infected with plague, the Spartans (mortal enemies of the Athenians) claimed that Pericles, the main political leader of Athens, was still polluted by murders committed generations earlier by his mother's family. The Athenians rejected the claim, but the Spartan ploy is evidence of how powerful the notion was.[4]

As the city suffered, Athenians began to blame Pericles for his hubris and inability to effectively meet the Spartan threat. He managed to push back, but ultimately Pericles, the friend of Sophocles, died of the plague, leaving a leadership vacuum. The vacuum resulted in partisan squabbling that weakened Athens, produced poor tactical decisions, and ultimately caused military defeat years later. Perhaps Athenians could smell their catastrophic fate in the dramatic action and narrative arc of Sophocles' choral complaints.

In 2017, the US was also experiencing a time of civil unrest. Donald Trump was inaugurated president in January. During subsequent months, his "America First" oratory brought intense value to some and distaste to others. In August, far-right, white-supremacist, and neo-Nazi groups demonstrated in Charlottesville, Virginia; Confederate monuments were removed from public spaces around the country; and Facebook announced that it had shut down hundreds of accounts created by a Russian company linked to the Kremlin that had created hot-button social issues during and after the 2016 US presidential campaign.

Flocking to the Athenian stage on the south side of the Acropolis every year for at least three hundred years would be seventeen thousand Athenians. They would come to watch plays by winners of the Dionysian theatrical competition. In about 430 BCE, Sophocles' *Oedipus the King,* considered the greatest of all plays by Aristotle, was performed, telling the tragic story of the unwitting Oedipus, whose destiny is to kill his father and marry his mother. Oedipus had first arrived in Thebes when the city was ravaged by an earlier plague. His arrival and marriage to the queen brought relief to the devastated city. He, as do the citizens of Thebes, assumes that he will have the same godlike power to purge the city once again. Instead, the soothsayer Tiresias identifies Oedipus as the true cause of the plague because of his crimes of killing his father and marrying his mother.

Flocking to the Las Vegas Village, a fifteen-acre lot used for outdoor performances northeast of the forty-three-story Mandalay Bay, were twenty-two thousand attendees on the final day of the Route 91 Harvest Festival, on October 1, 2017. The event had welcomed major country music acts to its stage on the Las Vegas Strip annually since 2014. Friends, families, and couples from around the world gathered to have some fun.

On the Greek stage and assisted by the impeccable acoustics of the amphitheater, actors projected their lines. Fifty chorus members that once surrounded the audience later appeared on a terrace by the amphitheater, enhancing the spectacle and the drama, most importantly here, with commentary.[5] The chorus "functioned variously as a physical extension of the audience, as the narrator of ancient myth, as an objective arbiter, as the extension of a particular character with whom it expresses solidarity, or else, as a fragmented group with diverse views."[6]

Just like the chorus, social media at the Route 91 Harvest Festival served as a platform to express what attendees witnessed and experienced. Everybody had their cell phone, taking selfies with friends, recording music, and sending videos and photos to friends and family. Attendees rejoiced in the sense of freedom. Once a ticket was purchased, the only loyalties, in this presumably safe space, were the friends of the moment. Country music lovers celebrated communal bliss within the carnival-like atmosphere, until 10:05 pm, at the peak of the revelry.

Right from the start of the play, the Greek chorus vocalizes both grief at the dying and political discontent with Pericles.[7] As the voice of the collective, the chorus expresses the first of Turner's three stages, the Separation stage, acknowledging the reality that the city can no longer sustain its normal daily life. As loved ones die, the chorus wails about the devastation of plague; their angst at ever surviving; their distress at the future of their city.

> Pain, misery beyond reckoning:
> My people, all my people, sick with plague.
> Search my mind for some defense,
> But there is none.
> No crops will grow, none from our fabled earth.
> No children crown the birth pangs of our women.
> . . . .
> Death, beyond the city's reckoning:
> Beyond pity, children lie on the ground unmourned,
> Bearing death to the living,
> While wives and gray-haired mothers
> Stream to the bank of altars,
> Exhausted by their sadness,
> Moaning, begging for relief. (168–74, 179–85)[8]

The chorus describes the catastrophe around them and over which they had no control.

On the final night of revelry, October 1, 2017, during the last set, at about 10:05 p.m., gunshots from a perch on the thirty-second floor of Mandalay Bay sprayed into the festival grounds filled with twenty-two thousand festivalgoers. Of the 445,696 hyperlinks tweeted within three days, the Separation stage tweets report the catastrophe with:

- 169,679 hyperlinks of major news source reports
- 51,306 survivor messages of life and death such as:
    I love you
    I've been shot
    I love you so much

In the same span, 529,310 tweeted images reported the developing tragedy:

- 271,002 information sources, including the Las Vegas Metropolitan Police Department and NPR
- 44,188 survivors in crisis

Social media provided the urgent communications necessary both for individuals and for the city of loved ones and support services.

On the Greek stage, after describing the grief, horror, and sense of impotence brought on by the plague, the chorus moves to the Liminal or Transition stage. In the Liminal stage, identity, truth, and power are all in flux. Accusations fly. The rush to resolution creates bitter discord. The chorus must address the cause of the plague. They are responsible for their city's well-being. In a state of denial, they cannot believe that their beloved king could be the perpetrator of death as the soothsayer Tiresias insists. They loved Oedipus and saw him as their savior from the previous plague. Choral voices express impotence and frustration at their own lack of access to information about the causes of this diseased catastrophe.

> And now I'm amazed! Worried. Frightened.
> That clever soothsayer—
> I can't believe him, I can't deny him, . . .
> No. I will not add my voice to the accuser's
> Until I see the charge made good.
> We saw him plainly—Oedipus . . .
> [when he ended the plague before]
> And we saw that he was clever.
> That was proof. The city loved him.
> I can't convict him in my mind,
> Not yet, not of any crime. (483–86, 504–11)[9]

They are moving out of denial and reluctantly determine their necessary judgment as the unwanted discovery of Oedipus and Jocasta's culpability looms.

At the Route 91 Harvest Festival, after the initial reporting of the tragedy, tweeted hyperlinks and images reflected the Liminal or Transition stage, trying to find the cause of what was happening. Survivors and those not at the festival tweeted included these hyperlinks:

- 140,009 Pro-gun control, politics, blame
- 32,732 conspiracy theories, hoaxes
- 13,485 debunking conspiracy theories

Shared images also cast blame, finding causes:

- 42,366 politics, mostly pro- but some anti-gun control
- 8,661 conspiracy theories or rumors

As festivalgoers and the community wrestled with the *why* and the *who,* social media allowed for the sharing of this flood of disparate ideas.

On the Greek stage, in the final stage, the Aggregation and healing stage, the chorus expresses the horror of what they have understood to be the truth. As certainty of the cause has become clear, the chorus can reflect on events, give them context, and look to a reconstituted status quo by reflecting upon a universal human reality.

> Behold, all you who dwell in Thebes: This is Oedipus.
> He knew the riddle's answer, he held great power,
> And we all looked on his success with envy.
> Now a terrible wave of trouble sweeps over him.
> There, always look to the last day,
> And never say a man is happy
> Until he's crossed life's boundary free from grief. (1524–30)[10]

Once the community voiced by the grieving voices of the chorus understands that the entire city of citizens has been affected by the catastrophe, that a cause has been discovered resulting in the cessation of the catastrophe, the chorus can now reflect on the shared experience, on the universality of grief, and on a city healing together.

A city mourns its dead but must tend to the business of the living. The visceral anguish of social media voices echoes choral voices in expressing reflections about life and prayers of comfort. Social media helped with medical assistance. In the Aggregation or healing and rebuilding stage, social media tweets included these hyperlinks:

- 30,258 victim funds
- 8,228 where to give blood

And finally, during the same period, in addition to prayers and words of support, an image appeared that identified the perpetrator. He was not a terrorist from overseas, but one of us:

- 52,083 *Family Guy* cartoon image marked as "local terrorist"[11]
- 49,567 compassionate wishes and prayers
- 32,256 where to get or give blood and get aid
- 25,444 service dogs
- 3,743 remembering a couple who died, "We should remember."

As Las Vegas began to heal, the actions of individuals and institutions sprang up to meet the challenge and join in the urgency to reestablish stability of daily life that would be forever changed.

The task of the witness, those who did not experience the trauma, is to help those who did and to remember the fallen while looking to the future. We are the witnesses, the chorus, the citizens of Southern Nevada. In analogous fashion, choral voices addressed, engaged, and shared with audiences, not as a separate but as a joined humanity transformed and transforming traumatic events and outcomes. By understanding the authenticity of Greek choral voices, we can better appreciate the essential service performed by social media in the face of the tragedy and ensuing trauma of 1 October.

NOTES

1. Victor Turner, *The Anthropology of Performance* (New York: PAJ, 1986), 25, 101. Also Victor Turner, *The Ritual Process: Structure and Anti-Structure* (Ithaca, NY: Cornell University Press, 1977). In chapter 3, "Liminality and Communitas," Turner points to the stability of the society from which the Separation springs creating the Liminal and finally the Aggregation stages.

2. During a personal interview, he provided the Excel spreadsheet documentations. See Thomas Padilla on UNLV Lied Library website: https://www.library.unlv.edu/about/staff/padillathomas.

3. T. B. L. Webster places its production in the Classical Period (450–425 BC) at about 430 BC, "slightly before or after." See *The Greek Chorus* (London: Methuen, 1970), 139. See also Pickard, *The Theatre of Dionysus,* 47.

4. David Wiles, *Greek Theatre Performance: An Introduction* (Cambridge, UK: Cambridge University Press, 2000), 42–43.

5. Graham Ley does a lively job of reminding us that the Greek taste in theater could be analogous to our taste for musicals. See *The Theatricality of Greek Tragedy Playing Space and Chorus* (Chicago: University Of Chicago Press, 2007). See also Lillian B. Lawler, ed., *The Dance in Ancient Greece* (Middletown, CN: Wesleyan University Press, 1965); and *The Dance of the Ancient Greek Theatre* (Iowa City: University of Iowa Press, 1964). See also David Wiles, *Greek Theatre Performance,* 13–14.

6. Wiles, *Greek Theatre Performance,* 125.

7. Wiles, 62.

8. Peter Meineck and Paul Woodruff, trans., *Sophocles: Oedipus Tyrannus* (Indianapolis: Hackett Publishing Company, 2000).

9. Meineck and Woodruff, trans., *Sophocles: Oedipus Tyrannus*

10. Meineck and Woodruff, trans., *Sophocles: Oedipus Tyrannus.*

11. Caricature of Peter Griffin, the main character in the sitcom *Family Guy,* appearing with the words "local terrorist."

5

Shock, Heartbreak, and Remembrance

University Medical Center, FEMA, and the Healing Garden

CAROLYN GOODMAN, Las Vegas mayor

Sam Mirejovsky and Amanda Signorelli (filling in for Ash Watkins) of the radio talk show *What's Right with Sam & Ash* interviewed Las Vegas mayor Carolyn Goodman on the fourth anniversary of the tragedy. Below is an edited transcript.

The call from [City of Las Vegas communications director] David Riggleman was quite a shock because I was fast asleep. It was Sunday night, and I was getting ready for an early Monday morning. The phone rang about twenty-five minutes after ten. David was on the phone and said, "We have no idea if this is a terrorist attack, how many people are involved with the shooting occurring at the [Route 91 Harvest Festival] site. And I'm calling to let you know and follow the protocol now." By the protocol, he meant back when I took office in July 2011, the first thing we did, seventy-two of us from Southern Nevada went to Emmitsburg, Maryland, for FEMA (Federal Emergency Management Agency) training. What we were doing for a whole week was training in terrorism and terrorist attack.

And when you have these types of organized, reactive protocols, you have a job—whoever you are in whatever area you serve—and you stay with that job. You do not interfere doing something else. So, my job, when I woke up, everything came immediately back, and I knew I was to wait for the directive to go to the central clearing for the city. But the phone call never came, and I'm an impatient person. When I didn't hear back within the protocol to me of ten, fifteen minutes, I knew I had the sheriff's cell phone [number]. I called him and said, "We live a block and a half away from the [region's only] Level 1 Trauma Center. Do you want me to go [there]?" And his only word was "Yes." So I was at the University Medical Center's Level 1 Trauma Center within fifteen minutes.

And, oh, my gosh. Oh, my gosh. Talk about the reality of that night. [We were] still without a grasp of what it was. Were there many? Were there problems at the dam? Were the hotels being blown up, or what was it? And finally word came in. Most importantly, the head of UMC had gone ahead and put out a [virtual] all-points bulletin: everyone came in, their crews, their maintenance crew, the doctors, the nurses. We even had doctors from Nellis [Air Force Base] and Sunrise Hospital coming over. People were being brought in on flatbeds [and other vehicles] by rescuers in the hopes the wounded would survive.

People with bloody arms, legs, and necks [who needed urgent care to survive] were rolled to the emergency entrance. They'd have five and six on a gurney and wheel them into one area or another to try to do everything they could. What was a miracle is that every admitted individual that night survived. Some, of course, arrived at the emergency and had already passed away. It was just unbelievable.

We had chaplains there and different faith leaders come in. One in particular, the person from the hospital, said, "Well, we have people in the room right outside here, who they don't know yet, but they have lost the person they were with, and they're in here just waiting for word. Will you go in and talk to them?" That was incredibly awful. I can't even begin to tell you.

The following morning, of course, we were all over at [Las Vegas] Metro [headquarters]. At that time, I was fortunate to have the microphone for just a few moments, but that was my job through the FEMA training to be the voice that was communicating. My only thing I could say was, "Give blood." These people were losing blood, and we needed blood. Within an hour's time, we are hearing from the blood banks: "We can't handle the numbers of people. We don't have the equipment. We don't have the technology. Please tell them to come back tomorrow, the next day, but don't go to the blood banks now."

For those who did come into UMC Level 1, [UMC] managed to save every one of them. Not that some didn't have lingering problems and issues, which beyond the psychological, which everybody carries who was there and will for the rest of their lives. And [some survivors], of course, lost people [close to them].

But beyond that, what was amazing to me, which I caught up with later on, was with [landscapers] Daniel Perez and Jay Pleggenkuhle. And, on a napkin, they drew up what they thought would be a wonderful thing for people to do. Anybody that knew anything that night, when they couldn't give blood and couldn't do something physically active—physically active—not give money. I mean, that's not the same. There was a need to touch, to connect, to do something.

Jay, Daniel, [then Las Vegas city attorney] Brad Jerbic, and Tom Perrigo from our Development Office got together very early that next morning and came up with a plan to build a [memorial] garden quickly. The city just gave a piece of property [at Casino Center and Charleston Boulevards], and over four hundred volunteers worked around the clock for four days and built this Healing Garden, which has fifty-eight trees in it, one for each of those we lost [that night]. And then there's the magnificent center tree, which was donated by [magicians] Siegfried and Roy. That is the center heart of the Healing Garden. Here we are four years later, and every one of those trees is more beautiful and bigger. And life, *life,* remembrance, is there. And that's where we will be connecting to those we lost.

God bless their souls. May they rest in peace. And our prayers and love go out to the families and friends of those we lost.[1]

NOTES

1. Carolyn Goodman, interview by Sam Mirejovsky and Amanda Signorelli, *What's Right with Sam & Ash,* Oct. 1, 2021; https://www.youtube.com/watch?v=1qa1Uui8Cew.

.

Part Two

PROCESS

The tragedy of 1 October reinforced how interconnected UNLV is with Southern Nevada. Our faculty, staff, and students wanted to know how they could help, and some had a direct role in responding to the crisis, offering medical and psychological care to those impacted. We immediately opened the Thomas & Mack Center as a shelter for the victims and assisted further by providing ongoing medical, professional, and technical expertise in the following days, weeks, and months. . . . It was an experience none of us will ever forget and was a stark reminder of how fragile life is and how much we love this community.

—CHRIS L. HEAVEY, Executive Vice President and
Chief Academic Officer, UNLV

The date that sticks out to me the most isn't October 1. It is October 2. Never have I seen the UNLV community come together as much as I did on that day. We all arrived on campus not knowing what to do, but knowing we needed to do something. The following organizations didn't rest for three straight days making things happen: CSUN (Consolidated Students of UNLV) student government, Student Involvement and Activities, the Graduate and Professional Student Association, the Rebel Vets Organization, the Division of Student Affairs; and the UNLV Administrative Faculty Committee. By October 5, we had sold more than two hundred Vegas Strong T-shirts to raise more than $3,000 for the 1 October Survivors fund and collected an entire U-Haul truck of supplies for first responders, medical personnel, and victims' families. We donated all materials to Forgotten Not Gone, the Red Cross, and United Blood Services for distribution. This was a dark time in the Las Vegas and UNLV community. We didn't know how much we needed to come together until we were done. And when we were done, the flood of emotions came over us all and we were able to grieve but also celebrate our community and come together to do good.

—SAVANNAH BALTERA, Director of Student Involvement and Activities, UNLV

6

Searching for Light

A Diary of the First Twenty-two Hours

MYNDA SMITH, sister of Neysa Christine Davis Tonks, 1 October victim

The phone rang about 11:45 p.m. on October 1, 2017. And life stopped. My nephew, Greysen, who was 14, called me after I had just returned home to Las Vegas from an exciting weekend with my oldest daughter, Hayley, in Denver, where I had taken her to see the musical *Frozen* for her early twenty-first birthday present. We had enjoyed a fabulous weekend together, and I came home exhausted. I awoke to Greysen screaming through the phone and saying his mom was dead. *What?* I couldn't understand it. He didn't understand it. He was yelling she'd been shot. So much confusion! I couldn't even take it in. My husband, Freddy, is now awake, and we aren't really talking much. Just frantically trying to head over to Glade's (my sister Neysa's ex-husband and the father of Braxton and Greysen). This was about getting to those boys as fast as we could!

Greysen had tried to call my mom and dad, who were vacationing in Wisconsin, but they hadn't answered. That's one of the first tender mercies in this mess. I called them and woke them up after I hung up with Greysen. They said the phone had kept ringing as they slept, but they didn't want to answer it until the third time when their guts finally told them something must be wrong and to answer the call. It must have been almost two in the morning in Wisconsin. They'd been there about a month in their new motor home and were planning to drive back to Las Vegas in a week or so. I think Mom answered, but I can't for sure recall. I do remember the screams. Screams from both Mom and Dad. They couldn't talk. I had no information for them. I told them I'd call them from Glade's. They just kept screaming, "No, no, no!" I don't think those screams will ever leave my soul. No one should have to get a phone call as horrific as this, nor make that call.

We drove to Glade's with so many questions. But I mostly was just confused. I had no idea what was going on! We pulled up to Glade's house, only a few minutes away, and the house was quiet. Eerily quiet. Greysen came out first. He was crying, but we were all in disbelief. How? Where? Why? I hugged him as long as he'd let me. I felt his heart break. Neysa's friend Ken (who initially received a call about the shooting) was there. Glade's brother and his girlfriend were there, too. Someone told us about the shooting. Some of the guys were getting information on their phones and possibly a TV in the other room. We heard two were dead. I couldn't believe Neysa was one of them! I remember thinking how could it be that she was one of two dead! My 17-year-old nephew, Braxton, came in. His hand was bleeding. He punched either a door or wall when he found out his Mom had been killed. He was hurt and still so upset. He didn't really want to talk, didn't want to be comforted. Kaden, my 24-year-old nephew, came in from another room. He let me hug him briefly. He was so distraught! He had been on a first date with a girl, Paytne, when she had gotten a call from her brother asking her if she was at the concert since he had heard about the shooting. She told Kaden about the shooting, and he started calling Neysa, knowing she had been there but thinking she had left by then. He called over and over with no answer as they headed straight over to the younger boys' dad's house (Kaden lives on his own). He had called Braxton, who also knew nothing about the shooting. On the drive over, he kept calling Neysa's phone and finally someone answered, telling him she had found Neysa's phone on the ground at the concert. By then, they had arrived at Glade's and everyone was outside crying and screaming. Kaden found out Neysa had been shot and killed, and he started punching the window of his car, so hard that his date thought it would break. What a horrific moment in time for them! How could they even process any of this? Especially since we had no idea what was going on! These three boys just had their entire world ripped away from them! Kaden's date had been talking with the lady who had Neysa's phone (her name was Kaylie) to calm her down. Her husband had been shot in the stomach, and she was very upset. She also said that Neysa's phone had blood all over it, which Paytne didn't tell Kaden about at the time since he was so upset. I never saw Paytne at Glade's house since she stayed in the car all this time. She saw us pull in and run into the house, but she didn't know who we were and didn't feel it appropriate to come inside. She said she waited for about thirty minutes with another friend of Kaden before she asked for him to take her home. Kaden later told me when he had spoken to Kaylie she had told him she had collected about six or so phones, and Kaden thought she said she was at "Green Valley Hospital," since she said her husband had been shot in the stomach. Kaden wanted to go find her. He wanted to drive there. None of us wanted him to go. None of us would let him go. He was ready. He wanted to find her. Find her phone. We were all so helpless and wanted, no, *needed* to do *something,* but yet we could do nothing but stand in the street in confusion and sadness.

I called my brother, Cody, and woke him and his wife, Jenni, up. I don't remember anyone crying. It was all a crazy dream! We were all so confused and shocked. I told Jenni I'd call with information. Cody didn't or couldn't talk to me.

The few times I called them that night, Cody didn't speak with me. He had Jenni talk. I know he couldn't take this overload of overwhelming information! I had to keep our conversations short because I felt I needed to help the boys. There wasn't much to say anyway. We hardly knew anything.

Trying to find the next words to say to my parents, knowing how each word I would have to say to them would crush them, was the hardest thing. No one but me was able to give Mom and Dad information, yet I had none to give. I wanted them to know everything we knew, though. I wanted to find information for them! Freddy was trying to get information. I asked him to call Rick, the father of one of our oldest daughter's friends, since he's a police officer. Rick didn't answer, but he did call back quickly. He didn't know much, but at that point had heard twenty were dead. *What?* She was one of twenty? He told me to get ready because that number was about to double real quick. *What?* Neysa was one of forty? I just couldn't understand it all! As we waited for information, the number kept rising. The guys in the room were getting constant information, either on their phones or a TV that I never saw. They were trying to protect the boys from it all. I never saw (nor have I to this day) any media coverage of that first twenty-four hours. I'd like to go back one day and watch it. To see and feel the rawness that everyone who was on the outside of the immediate tragedy felt, just as I was for 9/11.

Neysa's friend Marco had been with her at the concert. We heard he had been shot, too, and was at the hospital. We heard he'd be okay, but that was all we knew. My heart broke for him! We were waiting for him to call back with any information he could share about Neysa. Marco had been the one to call Ken after the shooting, and Ken did a conference call with Glade. Ken told Glade of the shooting and of Neysa's death. None of it made sense, though. We also heard that Glade's brother had spoken to a nurse who had been with Neysa after the shooting. Her name was Mary Ann, and we tried calling her but she wasn't answering. There were still no answers, and only more questions and confusion. The quietness was so unnerving. Once in a while, someone would cry. I went outside quite a few times to cry. Possibly scream. I still can't believe none of the neighbors ever came out.

Marco finally called; I'm not sure with whom he spoke. He explained how he had been with Neysa when she had been shot. How they had finally carried her out of the venue on a table since they didn't know if the shooting would start again. The thought of them carrying her on a table was overwhelming and just too real. I called Mom and Dad, told them to sit down. More screams from them. My heart fell apart as I heard their cries. I heard their friends try to comfort them yet knowing there were no words of comfort. It broke me that I couldn't give them any words of comfort, either. That I couldn't hold them and try to take some of their pain away. I was only relaying the most horrific information to them over and over again. I wasn't sure how much more of this I could give them. Having their friends Tom and Patty with them was something for which I am so thankful. Every time I'd call to give an update, I could just hear the screams. Somehow, I know they are on the floor, but I can't remember if someone said something about them falling or if I heard the fall. How much more of this could my heart take? How much more could *their* hearts take? The only thing I could do was give the little updates I had and leave them heartbroken and in tears. Those calls tore my heart apart, yet I had to hang up and try to figure things out.

We were getting word then that there was an active investigation for possible multiple shooters and roads were shut down. We told Kaden there's no way he's leaving. He had been wanting to leave during all this to go get his Mom's phone. His friend had been waiting and was going to drive him around town to find the phone, but he finally left. Maybe someone spoke to Neysa's friend Marco again. We now found out he had taken her out of the venue to a parking lot. They had stayed there until her friend was taken to the hospital. Marco made sure her body was covered, so no one could take photos of her. He took her purse so no one could steal it. And he left a paper taped on the table with his number and maybe two other numbers. I called Mom and Dad again. This was the second-hardest phone call of the night. The image in my mind of her being covered by a sheet was one of my most horrific moments: We *knew* at that moment that she was for sure dead. I held it together, though. Or at least as much as I could. All hope left me at that moment, and I knew it would be the same for my parents. It was. They screamed again when I called them. It was horrible! I tried to talk. What do you say? All I could do was listen. Listen to their screams. Their "No, no, no" over and over again. They had to get to Vegas, and they had to get here ASAP. Their friends called the airlines, and Delta had a flight in just a few hours. Two first-class seats were left. My parents raced to get on the flight. They had no luggage, just a small backpack and enough emotions to drown them.

Neysa's friend was now in the hospital, and we had so many questions. The nurse who had stayed with Neysa had Ken's number and had called him. They had made her leave the area where Neysa was, and she had no information for us on Neysa. Now we were lost. Where was Neysa? What did we do? Cody and Jenni were in Utah and couldn't do one thing to help us, which was incredibly hard for them. All they could do was watch the news to see what's going on. Sadly, because of this, I think they watched too much. They were thrown too deep into it all. They watched every second play out, knowing Neysa was in that mess, yet they, too, were helpless. It's all they could do, though, and I understand that. I just wish they could have been with us.

We were just standing around, cries breaking out every so often, but having no idea how to find her. Nanny and Bobby (what the grandkids call my parents) called and wanted to talk with the boys. At one point it was the boys, Freddy, and I outside in the street. Freddy started telling funny stories about Neysa. I was kind of annoyed at first, thinking how could he just casually tell stories of her when my soul was crushed and hurting so badly. I watched, though, and as he started talking, the boys were able to leave the chaos, if only for a moment. Maybe they enjoyed hearing the stories. Maybe it took their minds off their pain. One story in particular was when Freddy and Neysa got in a whipped cream fight at our house. Not sure who was chasing whom, but they were running through the house with a can of whipped cream! I reminded them all of the stain that is still on one of my linen chairs that often reminds me of that moment I wasn't so happy with! We laughed. It was a nice break.

Freddy reminded them to think of her life. Of her love. It was a nice moment. It seems about ninety minutes after we arrived that Cody saw on the national news that anyone in search of a loved one needed to go down to the Las Vegas Metropolitan Police Department headquarters. We knew we needed to get down there ASAP. We decided that Glade would drive the boys and follow Freddy and me. The roads were empty. It was maybe 1:30 a.m. Everything was quiet and dark. I don't remember talking much.

We arrived, and police were everywhere. We parked, and two officers searched us. I'd definitely never been searched like this. While it was strange and uncomfortable, it was a huge eye-opener about the magnitude of what we were dealing with, and I was grateful for the sense of security it brought. We walked in and found a huge room with many long tables. There were no colors or posters, just a plain room. I saw a table up front with some water bottles and a few snacks. Volunteers were walking around, and a few groups of people were sitting at tables. It must be a conference room where police officers gather for briefings and such. I told the boys this would be one of the worst things we would ever go through. That they needed to prepare themselves for what we might see and hear here. I knew people would be finding out their loved ones had been killed, and I wanted the boys to be prepared for the heartbreak we'd have to continually live through. Turns out we couldn't have been prepared for the heartbreak that was to come.

We walked in, and an officer told us to take a seat at a table. A few volunteers and police staff kept coming up, asking us why we were there. They asked for a description of Neysa so they could help us find her. We were asked this maybe ten times during my stay there. We then waited. More people came in. It was so quiet, but then a group of people in the back of the room started screaming. A horrible scream that hits the depths of your soul. I told the boys to cover their ears and try to block out the screams. The sick feeling in my gut told me they must have just found out their loved one had been killed. I figure most of us there probably didn't have good news coming our way. I wished I could have comforted those crying, but I sat trying to comfort the boys as they tried to drown out their screams.

We sat for a long time. I asked if they could get Braxton some ice for his hand. They just had cases of water bottles, so they grabbed the plastic from a case and somehow found some ice to place inside. It wasn't great, but it was something. I don't know how much he even used it. I was all over the place. I'd leave to cry. Leave to call Mom and Dad. I wanted them to have all the information they could possibly have. I even sent them a photo of the room so they could see where we were. Possibly even *feel* like they were there with us. I wanted so badly for them to feel like they were with us. I know they were so lost and felt so alone.

More people were arriving. More volunteers came. Then more and more screams? The more people who came, the more heartbreak it brought. Some came in, cried, and left. I don't know why. There were mostly just cries followed by silence. I think everyone was trying to be respectful of others. But most of us were there waiting. Sitting impatiently. Trying to pass the time patiently, but how? I didn't even get on social media. I don't remember it being a conscious decision but more of an inability to sit. I was trying to get answers. All of us were. Eventually, we stopped asking questions. The questions were pointless. Maybe because I knew she had died, it didn't make me interested in the "Why? Where? How?" My one objective was to find her. To take care of her boys at that moment. I was definitely in charge. I think I took charge the second I hung up with Greysen at 11:45 p.m. I probably offended someone along the way. I hope I also took pressure off some of our group to not have to worry as much. I know Glade was heartbroken and since he's the ex-husband probably didn't know where his place was in it all. But he's Greysen's and Braxton's dad and was a current friend to Neysa. He belonged there with us, and I'm grateful for him being there and all the love and support he brought.

My heart wanted to go around to each family there. Connect with them. Hug them. Find out whom they were searching for. Our hearts needed to come together, but we couldn't. Our journeys were individual journeys even though they were all similar journeys.

More and more snacks came. The boys welcomed some food. I didn't want anything, I couldn't eat. My mind was racing too much. My emotions had me on a wild roller coaster! We had been there for maybe ninety minutes before they finally told us they'd received information from the hospitals of names of injured who had been finally checked in. Up until that point, it was a city of chaos. The injured were overwhelming hospitals. So many were injured quite badly. We heard blood was everywhere in the hospitals, and people couldn't even get checked in. I truly hurt for everyone who had to live through that. I didn't really know at this time all the people who had been affected. I didn't know where the festival had been held. We hadn't heard of a shooter firing out of a window at Mandalay Bay. I didn't know the magnitude of the more than twenty-two thousand people running for their lives. The people who'd put themselves at risk to help those running. And I definitely couldn't wrap my head around the more than forty dead at that moment. We just sat there on our journey—our journey to bring Neysa home to us.

It was finally time for the names of those we assumed were being treated in hospitals to be read. We all gathered at the front of the room. I think the Metro officer's name was Charlie. He had been so nice to us, asking us many times if we needed anything. He tried to answer our questions, even though there were never any answers. He started reading. All of us gathered in front of him. Our hearts begging for our loved one's name to be read. I took a photo again to send to my parents. There was such a desperation in the photo. Such longing to find the loved one each of us was searching for.

Different hospitals had sent in lists. There might have been fifty names. It was pure silence. No one spoke. Our hearts listened intently to each and every name. We waited as he read each name, hoping our loved one's name would be read. *No one* was able to claim a loved one. Not *one* of us. We each walked away completely deflated. I'm certain those names had been mostly the injured who were able to call their loved ones, or someone was able to call for them, at some point, and were people whose families were not in the room with us. Now we waited again.

I did talk with a few people in the room. It was awkward, though, because everyone was so distraught, and I didn't want to get into anyone's business. One mom was looking for her son. She also knew he had passed away and was just looking to find him, like we were with Neysa. I then met a dad who said his daughter was in the hospital, but that they knew she was alive. They weren't allowed into the hospital since it had gone on lockdown. They were just trying to get information on how they could get to her. This was the only family I met who had some kind of knowledge that their loved one was alive.

We sat waiting and waiting. Nothing to look at. Nothing for the boys to think of. I think the boys were playing a game on their phones. We still weren't looking at the internet, which I now find so strange. Why didn't we choose to look at the phone to get any kind of information? Maybe my husband was checking his for information? I just kept trying to keep my composure for the boys, entering the hallway at times to lose all control of my emotions, and calling my parents to try to keep them in the space with us. Their friend informed me that they had booked a flight on Delta to come to Las Vegas and that they'd be arriving in Vegas by 8:30 a.m. I still don't know how that was able to happen, but I'm grateful for this ability for them to join me on this part of the journey. I only learned later the heartbreaks of their journey home.

We were thinking it was time for the boys to leave, but then Marco called to tell us he had checked himself out of the hospital and was coming to the police headquarters. He arrived about four o'clock, in scrubs with some blood still on his face and obviously looking exhausted from all that had transpired. We all moved to the side of the room, trying to get away from everyone, moving the folding chairs to form a circle. He wanted to share with us some of what had happened. He explained how they had been in the VIP booth section on the side of the concert. Neysa had on jean shorts, a pink tank, cowboy boots, and a cowboy hat. She had wanted to get in on the action and go to the floor. (She always wanted to be in the action!) It was an outside country concert, Route 91 Harvest Festival, and she loved being where the excitement was. She wanted to attend almost any genre of music events. I didn't even realize she was a country fan, but she was also a fan of heavy metal, pop, and a lot of '80s music! She just loved having fun!

When the shooting started, no one realized what it was, Marco said. Then it stopped. Everyone was kind of standing around, but word was spreading quickly that it wasn't just fireworks or problems with the speakers, like everyone was originally thinking. Then the sounds started again, and everyone started screaming to get down. Word was spreading quickly that it was a shooter. Everyone started to get down. People were falling. People were screaming that people were getting shot. The shooting stopped again, and Neysa did not want to run. She said for her and him to stay down. Her friend wanted to run. I imagined a small argument erupted of what to do when the third round started again. Even though Neysa was about five feet tall, she won most arguments, and this was no different. She ducked down, and he wasn't going to leave her, so he got down, too. They sat while shots were flying everywhere around them. Then it stopped. Marco told Neysa that it was now time to run, and he wasn't taking no for an answer. She didn't respond. He looked and saw her hunched over. He picked her up and saw a lot of blood. He realized quickly she had been shot and that she was struggling. He tried to get her to stay with him. He told her to fight for her boys. He kept saying how so many people loved her. How much her boys love her and for her to keep fighting. He said she died quickly, without much pain. Then the shooting began again. He stayed right there during all the shooting with Neysa. He laid on her during the stampede of people, his arms hovering over her to protect her. While Marco crouched over her, he was shot, with (he later learned) nineteen pieces of shrapnel starting from his armpit and going all down the side of his body. He didn't care if he was injured. He needed to stay with her and protect her. He said he had people stopping to help him. A few of them confirmed she was "gone" and moved on to help someone in need. They had some people who came to help take her out of there after the shooting finally had completely stopped. Marco had stayed there protecting her for all twelve rounds of gunfire! I can't even imagine the heartache and horror he saw as he sat there during it all. Some people helped carry her out of the venue and she was taken to the Desert Rose Resort, where many people had fled. A makeshift triage had been thrown together there to help anyone injured. Marco just sat with her after she was placed on the ground and was with her until a nurse, Mary Ann, saw him and asked if he'd been shot. She had been working on so many others when she had looked over and saw him hovering over Neysa. He didn't know if he had been shot. He lifted up his shirt, and it was apparent that he was shot all down his side. She and others made him leave for the hospital. He didn't want to leave Neysa. He begged her to stay with Neysa. She promised she'd stay with her until someone came for her. They found some paper and a pen and wrote some names and numbers on the paper—his number and possibly some of their mutual friends' numbers. I believe they taped it to the table she was on. He took Neysa's purse so no one could steal it.

He left for the hospital. The nurse said she stayed with her for about ninety minutes, before Metro came and said she had to leave the area. She told them about the note. She tried to stay, but they were clearing the area, and they wanted everyone out. This is when Neysa became a Jane Doe. Mary Ann was heartbroken when she found out this had happened since she had tried so hard to make sure that exact thing didn't happen, and, in the end, it must have been just too crazy for anyone to stop long enough to see the note.

I'm not sure what kind of treatment Marco got since he seemed to only be there a few hours. I'm quite certain he said he was fine and just wanted to get out of there to help us find Neysa. I don't think many people would have stopped him since they were so overwhelmed with medical needs from so many. He was now with us, though, and needed to help us find her.

We had tried calling Mary Ann, but she wasn't answering. At that time, we hadn't spoken to her, and we were hoping she could answer some of the questions we had. We thought she had been with Neysa when they took her away, so we thought she could tell us *who* had taken her. Little did we know the hell all those who ran from the concert were living in, too.

When Marco finished telling us as much as he felt appropriate for the boys, he asked if any of us had any questions. Greysen had a question. He wanted to know where she had been shot. How did his mom die. He took a deep breath and told us she was shot in the head. All of us started to scream. The screams overpowered this quiet room, filled with so many strangers. Some of them probably covered their ears now. I think a lot of people in the room thought we had just found out our loved one had been killed. Our screams were the same as those before us. It was a very hard moment for all of us. To think of her dying in such a horrific manner just broke us. We finally gathered our composure and stayed in a circle talking about what was next. Talk about what we could expect, but truly not having a clue what would happen in the days and months to follow. At this moment, I told the boys we needed to be strong. We would have so much darkness around us, and we needed to find light. We were sitting in the darkest moment I could have imagined right then. We all felt it. Everyone in that room felt it. An emptiness and sorrow that can't be measured but I *knew* there would be so much light to find, even though I had no idea *how much* there would actually be for us. We talked about the media, how they'd be after us. There was no way to prepare any of us for media! We told the boys not to talk to anyone without one of us there. We spoke of how people would be struggling with how to talk with us. Especially the boys and how they'd probably be asked stupid questions. How people would say stupid things. But how we needed to be forgiving of people's inabilities to find the right words since *we* couldn't even find the right words! The boys mostly nodded and agreed to everything. There was little conversation coming back as I spoke. The boys were still in shock. They were trying to process it all. We were *all* trying to process it all as our minds raced as we longed to find Neysa.

We knew sitting around this empty room filled with sorrow and despair was not healthy for the boys (nor any of us), so we sent the boys home with Glade. At this point, Ken was there, with Glade's brother, Scott, and his girlfriend. We all sat around. I cried a lot, but away from the boys as much as I could. Marco shared more about the shooting than he had shared with the boys. He then fell asleep. He was beyond exhausted. Freddy wanted to leave and go home, but I wanted to wait for the next reading of names. I had so much hope that we'd find her in one of the hospitals. All of us in that room were searching for *anything*, and I felt if we left, we would miss our chance at finding her. Any time someone came to speak, the room would quickly get quiet, only to be told there was no update. It was such a hard process to be at a place to receive information, yet they were receiving no information to give us. Finally, about 5:15 a.m., they read the names again. I think they read the old names plus new ones, but the result was the same. No one claimed anyone. Such heartbreak for all of us. With our heads hung, many of us were trying to map out our next move. Freddy said it was time to go home, wake up our daughters, and I knew that was the best thing to do. We had to go break the news to them, especially since our oldest was away at college. When I went to say goodbye to Charlie, a man was asking him to reread a name. Charlie searched the names and when he reread a name, which he had messed up the first time he had read the names, the man looked at his family of about eight people and yelled, "We found him." You knew they wanted to jump up and scream. To celebrate. They did a little, but I can't imagine how hard it was for them to be the only ones with good news in that room. They were mostly quiet and respectful to all those around them. It was the only name that was claimed while we were there. I was so happy for them. It was my first moment of light I felt. The joy wasn't for me, but it was still joy and light in that room of darkness. I was so grateful that *someone* had found their loved one. I didn't know the condition of the victim, but it didn't matter. They had him. As we walked out of the building to go home, that family was walking out next to us. I hugged them, and I told them how happy I was for them and that I was going to borrow some of their light until I could find some of my own. I think it made me feel a lot better to hug them—to try to absorb some of their happiness. I hope they felt my pure joy for them and that their loved one turned out being okay.

Freddy and I drove home. I couldn't call my parents because they were now on a plane to Vegas. I guess we were preparing to wake our girls and give them this most awful news.

We got home and called Hayley. It must have been almost seven o'clock in Salt Lake City, where Hayley was attending the University of Utah. It's hard to receive this kind of information when you're asleep, but we threw it all at her after waking her up. She was so confused and lost at what she was to do. She wanted to come home. We wanted her home, but we knew we had a long road ahead of us. If she could just finish the last few days of school, she could come home and be with us for her fall break. She cried, and it once again broke my heart in pieces. We then woke up Lexy, and we sat around the kitchen table. She was also confused. We also woke up the foreign exchange student who was staying with us, which made things a little more difficult. Lexy didn't cry much, and our foreign exchange student sobbed, causing me to give more attention to her than Lexy. I think Lexy was just stunned with this information, and I wish I had stopped to focus on her longer. To comfort her longer. To help her find her grief and sadness together. We gave them a few minutes and then told them to get ready for seminary (which is a church class they attend before school each day). We then woke up Kenzy. She was very upset. We held her and tried comforting her. This lasted just a little while before we told her to get ready for school. We had to find Neysa, and having the girls stay home would do no good for any of us. I wish I had the ability to hold each of them longer, to comfort them while they could comfort me at the same time.

I decided to go to Palo Verde High School to let the office know about Neysa and that Braxton and Greysen wouldn't be attending school for a while. Braxton was a senior, and Greysen was a freshman. As I walked into the garage to drive to the school, I found Lexy in her car, sobbing. She had called Hayley, and it had all set in. Seeing Lex cry alone in the car broke my heart, yet I didn't have the time to stop and console her like I wish I could have. I only quickly hugged her and left crying. I drove to the school, where I cried a lot. I told school staff members how Neysa had been killed in the shooting and how I didn't know what the next few days or weeks would look like. They were very sweet and promised they'd take care of everything. That they'd help me with *anything!* I left and headed straight for the airport to pick up my parents. The roads were still closed, especially the Strip, and so traffic was a mess. It took twice as long to get to the airport, but I was still very early.

I had been speaking with Delta Air Lines. An employee named Brandon had called, asking how he could help. He gave me all the information I needed to meet my parents. He said Delta was going to have a cart drive them from the airplane's gate to me in the concourse. He called me back and said he'd been calling the hospitals looking for Neysa. He said he had friends working in the medical field, and they were all looking for her. When he called me back a bit later on, he finally said he'd been looking for "Neysa Davis," and they'd come up empty-handed. I was so sad to tell him that her last name was incorrect. Davis was her maiden name! I felt bad that he had spent all that time looking for her with the wrong name, based on the names of my parents who were flying on Delta. He didn't give up, though. He just started again and called me multiple times. He was such a nice man, but he had no luck finding her.

I arrived at the airport and went to Delta's ticket counter. The agents there of course weren't aware of who I was or why I was coming, so they made a few calls. An agent found out what was going on and said she'd wait with me. I cried some more as we stood. If people were looking at us, I didn't notice. We just stood there waiting. Not long, though. We finally got word they were bringing my parents. When I saw them, I ran to them. I both hate and love that moment. A moment of such sorrow but finally having each other to face this tragedy together. Hugging them was deeper and stronger than it had ever been before. My mom's legs gave out on her. She couldn't easily stand, so we had to help her. We had to take a few minutes to gather our emotions. The Delta employees were all so tender with us. I can only imagine the scene we made. It breaks my heart to even visualize it. It was the beginning of a long journey together!

The agent with them said he'd walk us to our car. We really didn't need help since my mom and dad just had a backpack, but he wanted to walk us anyway. I still truly didn't know the magnitude of all that had happened, which looking back now makes even more sense as to why they all wanted to help us. This wasn't just our tragedy. We slowly learned it was a tragedy for our entire city, state, the entire country, and beyond!

Now what did we do since it was still only nine in the morning? I told my parents I wanted to stop at Valley Hospital to try to find the woman who we thought would have Neysa's phone. Kaden said she was at "Green Valley Hospital," but since that is not the name of a hospital in Las Vegas, I thought I'd try Valley Hospital. We arrived, and police were everywhere. Media were around, too. We were told to go to the emergency entrance, and we easily entered. I spoke with the woman at the desk who couldn't have been nicer, but I just didn't have enough information. I only knew her name was Kaylie and that her husband had been shot in the stomach, but that didn't get us anywhere. No phone had been turned into security, and we were out of luck. I started to really think this woman and Neysa's phone were just a hoax. That this woman had just found her phone, answered it, made up a lie, and was keeping the phone. I started to not like her.

Freddy called to say the media had just announced that the Las Vegas Convention Center had become a Family Notification Center. Anyone in need of *anything* could go there for help. Counselors and the American Red Cross would be there. And most importantly for us, there would be the coroner. We really thought, as we drove there, they were going to be setting up a morgue, and we would try to identify her body (among the many others) at this location. I have no idea where that idea came from: We think it had been originally stated on the news report my brother heard, but of course, thankfully, that didn't happen. It was a horrific thought in our heads. I was beyond grateful when we found out this wasn't the case and that we wouldn't have to go from body to body looking for her like I had imagined we would be doing. The car ride to the convention center was filled with sporadic sobs, questions, and a few calls to our family.

We arrived at about ten o'clock to a mostly empty Convention Center. A big room was set up with tables with water, coffee, fruit, and some Costco food such as cookies and chips. We weren't hungry, so we went out to find seats. A woman approached us, saying the media had released the information too soon and that the facility wouldn't be opening until one o'clock. Now what were we going to do? I told Freddy not to come and that we were figuring out what our plan was. We just sat on this column that had benches all around, not having a clue what to do. Shortly after our arrival, the coroner showed up. The woman told him our situation, and he approached us. He was so nice. He said to just give him a few minutes to get things set up and then he'd help us find Neysa. He did say that if he forgot about us to make sure we found him and remind him to help us. Sadly, we never reminded him of our conversation, and he did forget about us. We don't hold it against him. He had to be everywhere at every moment. We are truly grateful for all he did that day.

As we sat and waited for something to happen, many people approached us as they arrived. A lot of people kept asking us for a physical description of Neysa to help find her. I'm not even sure about the roles of the people asking us for her description. Volunteers? Police officers not in uniform? A man approached us to offer religious counseling. It turned out he was a politician and a member of the Church of Jesus Christ of Latter-day Saints, to which I belong. He was very nice, but my mom and dad didn't really want to talk to him much. There were too many emotions happening, and having a religious talk wasn't what they wanted. He didn't stick around for too long. A woman asked us if we wanted blankets. We were so thankful to get a few since it was quite cold, and the blankets stopped a few of the shivers we experienced off and on. Therapists and even therapy dogs started showing up. I wasn't really in the mood to pet a dog, but I did to make the owner feel good. I'm certain the dogs helped many people who came there that day, though. It just wasn't what I wanted or needed at that time.

A young man in his early twenties sat near us. He was completely distraught. We approached him and hugged him. His girlfriend had been killed while he was with her. I cried with him awhile. He was looking for her, just like we were looking for Neysa. We parted, wishing each other the best in finding answers. To this day, I don't know who he was or who his girlfriend was.

My parents and I had spoken of making a post on Facebook after we found Neysa. We didn't want to do anything before we knew 100 percent that she was gone. It was still too hard to wrap our thoughts around the idea that she had been killed. However, as we sat on those benches taking turns having emotional meltdowns, I saw a text come in. I had been receiving so many texts that I hadn't been paying attention to any of them. People texted to check in and make sure no one from our family had been harmed, but I couldn't stop to look at my phone at that time. It was so overwhelming. But I happened to see a notification that came in from Facebook that said, "I'm so sorry for your loss." *What?* Someone posted on Facebook and tagged me? Now, I opened up Facebook and saw comments like, "Please tell me your girls weren't there." I now saw texts with the same comments. Word had gotten out, and we needed to set things straight. We then made the heart-wrenching decision to make a Facebook post of Neysa's passing. Information was spreading like a wildfire, and we wanted the facts to be correct. This was one of the hardest things we've ever done! We sat and wrote it together. We cried as we wrote it, erased it, rewrote it again and again, and then finally finished it. I posted it and tagged all of our family, including Neysa. It was horrible. It was final. I hated it!

We sat there until about 12:30 p.m. For the first two-and-a-half hours, we just felt lost. People would talk with us and then move on. We were sick from the mental and physical journey we had already passed through. I don't even know how many times I'd just start crying uncontrollably. I wasn't angry. I was so confused and so sad. Overwhelmed. I still knew hardly anything about this horror. Just simple facts. More than fifty dead. I couldn't comprehend what was happening and that it was happening to us! I wasn't even really able to take it in. I wasn't looking on my phone for information or asking anyone what was going on. I had two goals: Find Neysa and take care of my parents. Taking care of my parents will always be one of the biggest priorities in my life!

We finally entered the big room in the Las Vegas Convention Center at about one o'clock, and all of a sudden *everything* had transformed! We could see cars pulling into a driveway at the far end—an endless number of cars coming in with so much food! I couldn't believe all of the food! Tables and tables of food. I walked over with my dad and opened the dishes up. Grilled chicken.! Hamburgers. Chicken fingers. So much! Then I saw a large fridge full of salads! It's mostly what my mom and I eat, so we were so grateful to have it to fuel our bodies. I honestly felt like I had run three marathons! We needed the food. We had all been up since just before midnight, and our bodies were starting to crash. We didn't eat much, but what we were able to eat was exactly what we needed. I'll never be able to express my gratitude to all those who helped make that happen. They showed such a great love for all of us so lost.

Freddy arrived shortly after. What I didn't learn until later was that he had been out looking for Neysa. He had gone to the site of the shooting but wasn't allowed to get close. The police had barricaded the area and wouldn't let him near. He then went to the coroner's office, where there was a police barricade, and he couldn't get anywhere close there either. I know I'll never understand the endless calls and places he went to that day, but I'm so thankful for him and his support. We had asked him to call as many people as he could to help us find Neysa that day. He tried so hard with no luck to find the right person to help us. I just won't ever know everything that he and others did that day, and that breaks my heart.

Freddy and I walked to the open area where people were dropping off food and supplies. We watched for a few minutes as car after car unloaded food and drinks. I wanted to thank the occupants of each car. I wanted to thank all of the volunteers who were unloading the food and setting it all up. Maybe some were getting paid, but my guess is that most of them were volunteers. There was so much love there that I kept having a hard time realizing that they were there for our family, those like us, and those who felt lost after witnessing the bloodshed at the festival. This was the first time since I received the call from Greysen the night before that I began to understand the magnitude of this massacre. I stood there with a firm realization that this was so much bigger. It scared me to think of all the things I didn't understand or know. I cried knowing there was so much heartbreak. There just had to be with this amount of outpouring of love. I was able to thank a few people before we walked away to find my parents again.

We ate, and the food tasted so good. It fueled us as we sat there at a round table surrounded by so many other round tables filled with people looking just as shaken as us. Freddy wanted to leave to try to do more to find Neysa, so I walked him outside where we hugged for what seemed like a long time. I really didn't want him to leave me, but I knew there was much to be done. I went back inside to find my parents sitting with empty looks, filled with exhaustion and such a deep sadness.

Glade sent us the name of an FBI agent who was at the Convention Center who would help us. We found him after being taken into a smaller room, and we finally started talking with people who we felt could help us. At this point, I think we had given Neysa's physical description more than fifteen times. After we were asked again, they were finally inputting the information into a computer, which finally made us feel like we were closer to finding her. This is when they started talking about Neysa's fingerprints. We didn't understand how they would match Neysa's fingerprint with a Jane Doe, especially if she had never had her fingerprints entered into a database. Only time would tell. We left feeling like we were no better off than before, but at least we felt like they had more information needed to find her.

The FBI told us it could be quite a while before anything would happen, so we decided to leave since my parents still hadn't seen Neysa's boys. We drove twenty minutes to Neysa's. We cried and hugged. I know the boys were grateful to have my parents there, just as I was. Upon our arrival to Neysa's, we were pleasantly surprised to find some of her friends who had come to the house. They wanted to clean it up and stock it with food for our family. I'm not certain how they learned of Neysa's passing, but I'm thankful they knew we would come to Neysa's needing food and a clean place to gather. We will forever be grateful to them for this beautiful act of service to our family while their own hearts were aching.

The boys were really struggling. None of us knew what to do, and waiting around made us all feel like we were doing nothing to find her. But there was nowhere for us to go, so we just waited.

Braxton had gone to school that day because of his commitment to sports. The Clark County School District rule is that if you miss school, you can't attend a game, and if you miss practice, you can't play in the game. Braxton went to school all week, while Greysen felt the need to stay home. Braxton must have felt great comfort being with his teammates and having the distraction of soccer. I'm so grateful he had that since I know it was a struggle for Greysen to not have anything to take him away from the sadness in which we lived each day. I know that having people around the house was enough to give him some kind of distraction; there was always some family member there to talk with or do something with if he needed.

I decided to leave and go home to finally change out of my oversize sweatpants and sweatshirt that I'd been wearing since the night before. I was a hot mess, with my hair in a bun, no makeup, and really grungy clothes. I quickly threw on a cotton dress and went back to Neysa's house. We were there for a while, trying to make sense out of this. At this point, it was about eight o'clock at night. We were so frustrated. We were all just lingering at Neysa's. Our younger of two daughters had come to the house with the foreign exchange student who was staying with us, and everyone was just sitting around on their phones. I had continually been calling the FBI. Freddy had been calling every politician he knew all day, asking for help. He reached out to anyone and everyone he thought might be able to help us. A friend who was a police officer was stationed at the festival site at this time. He said he saw her name on a list, so at that point Freddy was determined to get more information. We were still at Neysa's, but right about 8:30 p.m. Freddy said he was going down to the coroner again. There was no way he was going without me. Dad wanted to go, but Mom said she needed to stay at the house since there were a lot of people there and she didn't want to leave the boys. We promised Mom and Dad that we would call them right away if there was any chance of finding her. They made me promise that I wouldn't go in without them. I knew we all needed to do this together. I had no desire to do this without them! Kaden expressed that he wanted to come, too, but we all agreed it would be too much for the younger two boys. Freddy and I drove down to the coroner's, so hopeful but so scared. I didn't want this to be how it ended.

We arrived and found more police barricades. Police cars and officers blocked both entrances on the sides of the building. We approached and found two young officers. It was dark and still warm outside, but the lights lit up the area. We asked if we could speak with the coroner. They were polite but firm when they replied that they were instructed to let no one in. I begged them, and they said they were given instructions to keep people like us out and to send us to the Las Vegas Convention Center. I explained how we'd been there all day and how we'd given every bit of information we could possibly give. I showed them Neysa's picture. Mom and Dad had sent me a photo of her driver's license, so I had that as well as a photo of her from the night before, while she was at the concert. I told them she had three boys. I talked for a while about her. I now understood what the families of the victims from 9/11 felt like. I remember so many of them walking around the 9/11 site, begging for any information on their loved one whose photo they were holding. And here I was. Holding a photo of my loved one, begging for any information to find her! I felt like I had been transported onto the grounds of 9/11. The two officers kept talking to each other. I'm certain their hearts broke for us, but their job needed to take precedence over their emotions. We begged them. We just had to find out if she was here. It had almost been twenty-four hours since she had been killed. Where else could she have gone? One of the officers finally said he'd go speak with the assistant coroner. Could this be a little bit of hope we'd been searching for? We waited for a while before he came out and apologized. He said that she told him to send us to the Convention Center. *Ugh!* Another blow that felt like a punch in the gut! As he spoke to us, we suddenly saw the assistant coroner walking toward us. As she walked, my heart was racing. But my mind was telling me that she must have been preparing to bring us bad news, which is what happened. She apologized and said we had to go to the Convention Center where the coroner was. She said that he was the one we needed to see. I explained it all again. Freddy explained how he'd called everyone and how we had gotten nowhere with any of it. How we'd given her description over and over again. She said there was no fingerprint match yet, and we'd have to go back to the Convention Center. We explained how we kept hearing that her fingerprint was the key to finding her, but what if she'd never given her fingerprint in the first place? There would be nothing to match!

I turned on my phone and pulled up the photo of Neysa that we'd received from that night. She was in her brown cowboy hat, pink tank top, and blue-jean shorts with cowboy boots. This is what she should be wearing now, wherever she was. I then showed her a photo of Neysa's driver's license that Mom and Dad had texted me. I explained for the last time how she was one hundred pounds, and five foot, two inches. She had implants and a tattoo on her lower back. I explained how I'd said it so many times but couldn't understand how it had been so hard to find someone with her description? There couldn't have been that many women who looked like her who had been killed that night! I don't know if it was what I said or what Freddy did or said, but all of a sudden, she told us to hold on. She thought that she might have some information and that she wanted to take us inside. Really? Could we actually be getting information? Could we be finding her? I called my mom and dad and told them to get Kaden and rush down now. It seemed like something might happen. The assistant coroner went inside. When she came back out, she explained that she thought she had a Jane Doe that fit Neysa's description. I couldn't believe it! All this time searching with no answers and now it felt like we were so close! I started to picture Neysa in my mind. What she would look like after getting shot in the head. The picture in my mind was horrific. It should have made me physically sick. It definitely paralyzed me for a bit. I wondered if I would even be strong enough to do this. But my parents, my nephew, Freddy, we were all doing this. I am thankful Freddy was there for all of us. He is so strong. He made me strong. I tried to stay strong for this moment. For my parents. For Kaden. I figured I'd be the one who'd have to identify her since I didn't think my parents nor Kaden would be able to handle it. I spoke to my parents as they drove down. My dad said to get prepared for what we were about to find. That identifying her would be the worst thing we'd ever have to see in our lifetime. I said that there was no way it could be worse than what I had visualized already. We waited about fifteen minutes for them to arrive. Fifteen minutes of fear. Hope. Gratitude. Anticipation. More fear! Our friend was outside when my parents and Kaden arrived, and he had guided them where to go. I really appreciated that! I'm certain he was a warm face to them that brought comfort. We hugged with hope in our hearts, but much fear, too. A longing for this to all end. It was so sad to me knowing the inevitable, but longing for it. To heartbreakingly confirm her departure from this earth yet needing the comfort it would bring so badly. We sat in a small room around a circular table. No one spoke. We were so afraid. We were so not prepared to see Neysa after this monster took her away from us so violently, so cowardly. It was so quiet as we prepared ourselves to view a body that we prayed would be Neysa's, yet also knowing it could be someone else. We had fully understood that what we were going to see would be something none of us could ever prepare for and could haunt us forever.

The assistant coroner sat at the table and told us she'd be showing us three photos. *What?* Photos? We weren't going to identify her actual body? Just photos? I can't explain the shock that brought, but a full gratitude in my heart. For me. For all of us. I truly thought all along we were searching *for her* as we searched for her body. For the worst moment no one could ever prepare for. Now we just searched for her with the tender mercy of not having to see her actual body at this time.

She turned over the first photo. The tattoo. None of us responded for a few seconds. Then I said it wasn't hers. That it wasn't her tattoo. My heart sank. No, crashed. Kaden quickly said it was. We didn't really know what to think. Was it hers or something similar? It's crazy now to think that I would have even been able to say one way or another if it was her tattoo or not. I hardly saw it, except on pool days, and she really didn't just walk around showing it off. (She was usually sunning on a lounge chair taking a nice nap.) Mom later said she also knew it was Neysa's tattoo. I don't remember her agreeing with Kaden, although she might have. We didn't argue, though. The assistant coroner prepared us for the next photo by saying the woman's head had been wrapped in a white towel and we would only be seeing her face. They had cleaned her face, and her head injury would not be seen in any way. Another tender mercy! She turned the photo over and it was Neysa! Almost angelic to me. There was only, what I believed, to be was a little blood spot on her face. I cried a little. Mom gasped and then softly cried, and Dad cried a little, too. I think we all were in quite a bit of shock, but we were just so relieved to find her! To have her back! She looked beautiful to me! It was her! We had searched and searched for almost twenty-four hours, and now she was ours again. We gave the photos back. We just sat in silence for a bit. Frozen in that moment. The assistant coroner said how sorry she was. She was so sweet. She started doing some official paper-work. I asked if I could see the photos again. I felt so strange asking. Like it wasn't allowed. She gave me the photos, and I touched Neysa's face. It was like I was actually touching her! I cried some more. Then Mom and Dad asked to see it. And then Kaden. We all cried. We just sat holding her photos. Touching her face on the photo. It's weird, but it meant so much! The assistant coroner then asked who wanted to officially iden-tify her. I wanted to jump and say, "I did," but I didn't want to be disre-spectful to everyone else, so I said nothing. It was something I thought my parents or Kaden should do before me. No one else said anything though. We all just sat in silence. I'm certain my parents and Kaden were in shock. She looked at Freddy and said, "Well, I guess you can just sign for her." The word "just" jumped at me like someone coming in for an attack! That's when I spoke up. No! I wanted to! I wanted to sign for her and make her ours again. Give Neysa her life back. I don't know why that meant so much to me, but it really did. I had searched so long, and to have her back was everything my soul needed! Signing was empowering. That sounds crazy, but signing my name was so emotional to me. I cried as I signed, feeling a part of me was gaining her back. A feeling that we were whole again. That *she* was whole again. We sat as the assistant coro-ner finished everything up. We hugged her so much. We were so grateful to her. She gave us her card and we walked out, thanking her for all her help. We came out with a peace. It was such a feeling of comfort to know where Neysa was. To not have her be "lost." I guess looking back, I'm a bit surprised that none of us asked to actually see Neysa's body. It wasn't something I desired to do, and I suppose none of the others needed to either. For me, the photos were enough. As we walked down the sidewalk toward the car, I saw the police officers whom we had seen earlier. Later, I asked Freddy if I ran to them in my head or if I actually ran to them. Yep! I actually ran to them. I hugged them and thanked them for giving us a chance. Without them being willing to take a chance, to "break the rules," and to talk with the assistant coroner, we never would have found Neysa that night. I'm certain that a lot of people "broke the rules" those first twenty-four hours, and to all of them my heart is forever grateful. Their compassion over "rules" not only probably saved lives, but I imagine brought huge amounts of comfort and help to our city! I got in the parking lot with Freddy and said goodbye to my parents and Kaden. We all needed sleep, and they needed to return to Braxton and Greysen. My first call in the car was to Marco. I wanted him to know we found her. He didn't answer, and I was heartbroken. I wanted to talk with him and bring him some peace. I sent him a text. I hope it brought some kind of peace to him that night! My parents called my brother and his family. They needed to know all that had happened. They were so torn not being able to be here with us. Hayley, too. They were working on getting here ASAP.

We drove home, and I was exhausted. It had been almost twenty-four hours without sleep. My dad later said to someone it took one week to find Neysa, something which he struggles to let go. It truly did feel like longer than twenty-two hours of searching, both physically and emotionally. But I'm truly grateful that it did only take less than a day and that we were only searching for Neysa alone. I can't imagine if one of her friends had also been killed, or even if her boys had been with her, too!

I went home, though, and couldn't sleep. I got on Facebook and started to see all the messages I had received. I looked at some of my texts. There were so many. It was so overwhelming, but I had to read those I could. Somehow it fueled me. I should have slept, but I needed to feel the love of so many. I finally fell asleep about three o'clock, maybe four, and woke up at seven, ready to get started on all we needed to do.

7

Las Vegas Healing Strategies

Mementos, Family, and Acts of Love and Kindness

Claytee D. White, director, Oral History Research Center, unlv Libraries

I just wish we didn't have to go through tragedies
like this to regain our humanity.

—Stephen Round

How does an orderly society create a space for mass murder run rampant? The space was created long ago from many injuries. The wound is deep. We witnessed one of those moments of terror that deepened the tear in the fabric of our reality in our home, a space where we feel safe. Las Vegas is home and uniquely carves out places for tourists that allow us to be the Entertainment Capital of the World and yet let us live like we are in a small town. We see our governor at local events, our mayor at all kinds of programs, our children's teachers in grocery stores, our pastors in restaurants, and casino executives at parks. We are a community that is more reminiscent of family. And yet, one of our visitors, who did not know us, tried to murder our energy, our style, our sense of self. We mourned; we hugged tightly; we aimed back with love.

Nick Robone, a hockey coach at the University of Nevada, Las Vegas, grew up in Las Vegas and attended the Route 91 Harvest Festival with his brother, a firefighter, on October 1, 2017. The tickets were a family birthday gift for Robone, an act of love. That family used a similar show of love to help heal him. Robone was shot in the chest on 1 October. Telling and retelling the story acted as a healing vehicle for his wounds and his psyche.

A highly respected manager in Las Vegas valley water management systems and a ten-year educator with the Clark County School District, Christine Barrett recently discussed with me a new way of looking at the

valuable work of oral history. She believes that the *story* is the underlying element that supports the culture of all societies. As an oral historian, I collect stories, and I retell those stories at conferences, in articles,
in classrooms, and in public presentations throughout the city. Barrett
argued that there can be no dance, visual art, song, opera, drama, musical, or film without first a story. Robone used his story of his family's love
to heal his body and his trauma.

Stephen Round, on a staycation at Aria Resort and Casino in Las
Vegas, was acting as an unofficial tour guide for two ladies he met at the
Luxor. As they walked toward Tropicana Avenue, away from Mandalay
Bay, shots rang out. He told the tourists to run as he tried to determine
the source of the ricocheting shots that echoed throughout the vicin-
ity. No answers satisfied him. The next morning, as he learned more,
he found himself as close to the scene at Las Vegas Boulevard and Reno
Avenue as police allowed. As he and others congregated there, a makeshift memorial site began with representations of hearts, candles, flowers, and soon T-shirts and armbands with the words, VEGAS STRONG.
Round did not know how to feel as people left items and took photos of
each other as they placed mementos at the intersection. But then he discovered that the space had to be protected. Memories and stories needed
to be captured, so he ran to the nearest location open for business and
grabbed a small diary. Thinking on his feet, he asked people to sign the
book and jot down their feelings. He simultaneously discovered that he
needed to be at the site to make sure the sentimental and sometimes
expensive items were not taken by community members in need of life's
necessities. Round helped heal the city with these mementos and stories that eventually went to area museums. The diary is in Special Collections and Archives at UNLV. Newspapers ran stories about memorials
that sprang up around the city. People visited these places to heal and
leave items so others could heal. Round and others with his calling protected these sites and assisted a few days later in loading these mementos
on trucks to take them to places in hopes of saving them in perpetuity.

Charles Scott Emerson was the leader in an organization of service,
the local chapter of the American Red Cross. Las Vegas overwhelmed him
and his organization with its generosity. As he and his coworkers received
all the goods, they released them out to targeted locations of survivors,
their families, and friends. He healed the city with his sacred service. On
1 October, Emerson had just returned from Houston, where he had served

Texans trapped in the eye of Hurricane Harvey. After a few hours of sleep, his phone had pinged like those left on the festival grounds. He sped to his office and began to assist his city, his neighbors. Emerson's staff converted the Excalibur Hotel and Casino parking lot into a triage center. Callers to the Red Cross office offered to help, and others called with needs. The Red Cross matched the two. By the second morning after the tragedy, Emerson welcomed colleagues from across the country. Some had experience from the Pulse nightclub shooting in Orlando, Florida, others from the Boston Marathon bombing, and still others who had helped after school shootings in Newtown, Connecticut, and San Bernardino, California. Healing valves turned on from all over the country, spraying expertise, care, love, and experience all over Las Vegas.

Acts of love did not stop for weeks and continued at the shooting's anniversaries. Although the city has moved on in many ways, we still feel it. We have not forgotten to treat our neighbor as ourselves. Yes, even in the middle of the current political environment, it is possible to forget red and blue and just be family. Robone, though wounded, because of his peak physical conditioning in the hockey arena, permitted others to get into ambulances in front of him. "I really didn't know how serious my chest wound was, but other people were shot in the neck and in the head." Robone talked himself into breathing. "I knew I would give myself a better chance of survival if I just breathed and stay focused. I couldn't freak out."[1]

I am reading *A New Republic of the Heart: An Ethos for Revolutionaries* by Terry Patten.[2] Patten believes that we are on the verge of a catastrophic breakdown, and we will need guidance and higher wisdom. Robone showed that kind of guidance and wisdom on 1 October. To heal and remain in the healing flow, he took care of himself and others.

Round acted on instinct. He had never protected or contributed to a makeshift memorial. This was not the usual act of duty for him. In this instance, acts that he could perform instinctually, such as breathing, took the fore. This time, he exhaled out onto our city and became a revolutionary being, loving his Las Vegas neighbors as he had loved his countrymen over his long military career. He transformed his wild heart and cooled his mind as he entered the republic of the heart. Writer and thinker Patten "turns the black diamond of our global darkness to illuminate our hearts, hone our capacity for selfless service, and resplendently deepen our commitment to enact our divine identity and it joy, whatever happened."³ This stunning marriage of the wild heart and cool mind tugged at Round, Robone, and Emerson.

Emerson moved to Las Vegas in 2004. Because he frequently traveled, he could not get a foothold on friendships in Las Vegas like he had enjoyed in his small town in the Midwest. He says, "1 October was our natural disaster that pulled us together." After all, Southern Nevada does not have hurricanes, tornados, and 7.0 earthquakes. "I did not receive a single 'no' from anybody any time I asked for anything," Emerson says. Recognizing that the first Family Assistance Center being staged at the Las Vegas Convention Center was stark and impersonal, Emerson reached out to Michael Severino of Southern Wine and Spirits. Because Severino has connections, as his business card states, "I'm a guy that knows a guy," his florist sent tall trees that gave the area a grounded feeling of the earth though the ground was moving beyond reason. Emerson and his Red Cross coworkers set up stations that helped with driver's licenses, immigration issues, food and water, a play area and a trauma area for children, and other services that many people often don't think about.⁴ That's just what the Red Cross does. They loved their neighbor, gave mementos beyond T-shirts, and formed a new kind of family structure.

Robone, the hockey coach, went into surgery after he was finally triaged at Sunrise Hospital. He awoke to family from Las Vegas and other kin from across the country. He told his story to each person. The retelling was therapeutic.

When Barbara Tabach and I prepared to collect 1 October interviews about a month after the massacre, we first consulted a therapist. The therapist advised us to talk about the interviews as we collected them. The telling helps to avoid post-traumatic stress. Think about the hell of that evening's battlefield as one lone gunman targeted, killed, frightened, and traumatized thousands of festival attendees who were delighting in a glorious evening only minutes before. We will never know why this happened, but the healing began that very evening. The healing was at first intangible and quickly moved to tangible acts as passers-by took people to hospitals. People around the festival's perimeters took strangers into their homes. Casinos shut their doors to protect those who ran in to take cover. And doctors and nurses worked with no thought of themselves. They just put their training into overdrive and cried healing tears later.

I believe that Las Vegas went briefly into the *New Republic of the Heart.* Patten, who completed his book one year after 1 October, believes that the world is at a tipping point and that we are in big trouble—not just related to the climate and the biosphere but in every arena of human and nonhuman life on Earth. This means a collapse of the entire social fabric of the world.

That's pretty dire. As I look back over the last five years, Patten may be on point. But Las Vegas has a model of civility and love to reference. On the evening of and days after a horrible crime, the city reacted with signs of respect, honor, care, and love. Of the three men in this essay, Robone, with his chest damaged by the anger of a shooter, chose calmness and respect for his fellow man. Later, he told everything to his family, both those who live in Las Vegas and those who flew in from New York. The story was healing.

> From the time I woke up in that hospital bed after surgery and telling people about it and going and going and going, and I think that has helped me a lot with it. I didn't keep anything in. I literally have no problem telling anybody about it without getting emotional or anything like that. I think that the repetitiveness of it and bringing it up and reliving it and things like that, it just makes us say, *"Okay, this actually happened. I made it through."* I think that some people just hold it in too much, and they don't want to talk about it. They don't even want to think about it. They don't even want to see anything on it. But it was an event that actually happened, and you have to sometimes relive it to make sure. It's one of [those] things where you cannot learn from it, but realize that you went through it, you survived, and now what are you doing to help yourself and help others? That's what I've come out with, how can we help each other?[5]

But Rabone was not done. He formed an idea of how to pay back the care that he felt from people all over the city, especially the hockey community that had been good to him all of his life. He did it his way knowing that this idea would only be a token, a tiny memento of what he had received from his family, nurses, doctors, and the hockey world in Las Vegas, his city. He found home in the hockey community, in a relationship that had grown since he was a kid. He wanted to give back by organizing a public skate early in February 2018. All proceeds from the $10 entrance fee would go to post-traumatic stress disorder victims of Southern Nevada. The event would feature the UNLV hockey team, a raffle, and time for the community to skate. It was an evening of freedom and beauty and grace to commune with family, even those family members whose names one did not know. This is what family is and how it operated.

Helping to disassemble the 1 October street memorial with its myriad of mementos, Round found his way to Special Collections and Archives at UNLV's Lied Library. When he explained what his treasure was, he was sent to the department head, Michelle Light. As she listened to his account, she led him to the Oral History Research Center, where his memories were recorded and transcribed. Additionally, Light took the diary that Round had created to our Special Collections and Archives conservator, Michael Frazier, who constructed a special box to house it away from dust and from fingers roving along a storage shelf. During his interview, Round reflected on healing moments and mementos he had experienced:

> I'm not a hugging kind of guy but one day, there was a girl standing alone crying with a bandaged arm. I went up and talked to her. She had been shot at the concert. I talked to her a bit, and I asked if I could give her something. One of the Metro [Police] sergeants had given me a patch and a coin from an officer who responded that night. The officer wanted the mementos to go to a survivor if one stopped by. She pinned them to her armband. I walked her across the street where a Billy Graham [Rapid Response Team] crisis person was offering counseling. This was kind of what we kept doing. We would help if they asked and then walk them toward people trained to assist. Others, I offered the book to write something. A PA (physician's assistant) from Sunrise wrote: "Your loved ones did not die in vain. They were surrounded by friends, some they knew, some they didn't. Heaven has fifty-seven angels and one sheep dog to protect them."[6]

Emerson of the Red Cross also knew how to take care of Las Vegans and, in that caring, did not forget his own Red Cross people. His paid staff and volunteers created miracles, shifting us from fear to love. Just the idea of the deep listening was exhausting. We are a city of magic, wrangling supernatural forces. Emerson thought to wave his Red Cross magic wand and reach out to Cirque du Soleil, the premier performing company on the Las Vegas Strip:

Cirque du Soleil shows went dark on Monday night, October 2, and they resumed on Tuesday. What people don't know is Cirque du Soleil gave us almost two hundred tickets for our Red Cross workers to come escape what they were working with for ninety minutes. When I was having an e-mail exchange with their vice president of resident shows, he said, "What can we do?" I said, "I have a big ask. I have two hundred people here, and they need a break, and the best way to give them the break is to immerse them into your magical world of Cirque du Soleil. I don't need two hundred tickets to one show. It's actually best if you scatter them out because they all get in groups, and they want to go at different times and based on their work schedules and stuff." He said, "Whatever you need, we've got it."

We had a volunteer come in, and that's all she did was coordinate people going to the show to get a break. You have to look out for your own people, too. With Red Cross volunteers, we're not always so good at monitoring our own empathy and passion. This was a great way to kind of break that up and give them a little bit of an escape and have fun.[7]

The Red Cross has formed family all over the world since 1881. After 140 years, the Red Cross is still providing services to members of the armed forces and their families in addition to providing disaster relief in the United States and around the world. After 1 October, it was time for Las Vegas to witness this loving care up close and personally. The Red Cross did not disappoint. Along with other first responders, the Red Cross cradled the city, took us in their arms, and rocked us for a little while.

Now, five years later, we are ever awakening to the truth. In his book, Patten quoted Andrew Harvey, a British scholar and religious thinker, who stated, "When the deepest and most grounded spiritual vision is married to a practical and pragmatic drive to transform all existing political, economic, and social institutions, a holy force—the power of wisdom and love in action—is born."[8]

I believe the truth is that a reforming of systems is necessary, a revolution in thinking and behavior is necessary. We have gone too far into the abyss, the darkness, the nadir, the lowest point away from anything mirroring goodness, purity, love, peace, divinity, and spiritual grace. Shooters into crowds of innocence illustrate this. Our vast homeless population and the number of food banks in affluent countries showcase this. Inequalities in health care, education, jobs, housing, banking practices, police brutality, and criminal justice speak to this. The Las Vegas shooter, corrupt politicians worldwide, gunmen in Connecticut, Florida, California, Colorado, Texas, Great Britain, France, and throughout the world showed us that it is time for transformation. Symbols are not enough without the power of love. In the face of all of this, Patten believes that a new culture is spreading across the planet. Growing like a plant, underground and invisible, this new culture will flower.

Emerson knows that "Vegas is a town where the show must go on." And I agree. I also know that we have not completed our lessons from 1 October. Emerson, like Patten, thinks that we have a responsibility to get to know our neighbors and get to know each other and embrace each other and be one. We do. "That's the best thing we can do," Emerson says. "So, if people want to pour energy into something, pour energy into making a neighbor. When was the last time you actually went around and introduced yourself to your neighbors or hosted an open house for people to come by? Yes, you may only get one or two, but it's a start. That's how everything starts."[9] We've had five years.

Danny Cluff, a poet who attended the Route 91 Harvest Festival, read this to me as I completed his interview:

> Time has passed, so people ask if now I am okay. But my mind is scarred; therefore, it's hard for me to say that I am okay. I know through time I'll heal my mind and one day I'll be okay. But it won't come quick; the time will tick before I can feel this way. Some might take longer, but we'll all be stronger once we reach that day. It's a hard pill to swallow and tears will follow, but we will once again be okay. It won't be fast, the time will pass, might not be tomorrow nor today. We will reach that goal and then feel whole, and we'll feel better than okay. We still feel pain; our lives have changed; memories don't easily go away. We still hear the screams within our dreams haunted by the demons of that day. But as time passes, we'll rise through the ashes, and we will overcome that evil day. This evil, [we] will conquer, and we will be stronger. We will be better in every way. So life, live it up. There's no giving up. When you need help, you can pray. With every breath in you, there's fight left in you, and we'll fight until our last day. Together we can do this. I know we'll get through this. We won't let this evil have its way. So,

when the time has passed and that question they ask, you can answer you're better than ever that day. So, let's follow the trail that leads out of this hell. In the past these demons can stay. We'll do it together and be stronger than ever, and I promise we will be okay.[10]

NOTES

1. Nick Robone, an oral interview for Remembering 1 October Oral History Project, interview by Claytee D. White and Barbara Tabach, December 21, 2017, p. 7.

2. Terry Patten, *A New Republic of the Heart: An Ethos for Revolutionaries* (Berkeley, CA: North Atlantic Books, 2018).

3. Patten, xii

4. Charles Scott Emerson, an oral interview for Remembering 1 October Oral History Project, interview by Claytee D. White, December 21, 2017, 17, 18.

5 Nick Robone, 14.

6. Stephen Round, an oral interview for Remembering 1 October Oral History Project, interview by Claytee D. White, October 25, 2017, 21.

7. Emerson, 24.

8. Patten, 211

9. Emerson, 9

10. Danny Ray Cluff, an oral interview for Remembering 1 October Oral History Project, interview by Claytee D. White, December 8, 2017, 22.

8

Therapeutic Innovations, Outreach, and Lessons Learned

A Practical Guide for Community Response

TERRI KEENER, Nevada behavioral health coordinator,
Vegas Strong Resiliency Center

*Sometimes we need someone to be there with us—not to
fix the problem, not to offer advice, not to do anything in
particular—to simply be present with what we're feeling,
to show up and acknowledge what we're going through
and hold a supportive, safe space for us to
be with what's showing up for us.*

—AUTHOR UNKNOWN

October 1, 2017, was not much different than any other day for me. It was not until October 2 that I learned of what happened on that terrible night. Since then, October 1 each year will never be the same for me—and I wasn't even there.

I've lived in the Las Vegas area since 2004 since moving from a very small farming community in the Midwest. During our time here, we have not taken advantage of the crowded events and activities in the fabulous entertainment community where we have made our home. I was not even aware of the Route 91 Harvest Festival. Now it is something that I will never forget.

On October 2, 2017, my husband woke me up at 6 a.m. with the words, "Honey, you are going to be very busy today." At that time, I worked for Clark County and coordinated the crisis intervention team for one of its largest departments. His words were true for the days and months that followed.

Months later, when I learned of the behavioral health coordinator position at the Vegas Strong Resiliency Center, I was immediately drawn to the opportunity to become even more involved in an official capacity. While the VSRC had been in place for a few months, this was the first full-time position to be dedicated solely to the center. The new position, still being defined, carried with it a variety of duties–anything that seemed to be connected to behavioral health. When it involves the largest mass shooting in recent US history, when is behavioral health *not* a part of it?

Even with my experience working with trauma and people of all ages experiencing the worst time in their life, I thought it was important to acknowledge that I had a lot of learning to do when I started my new job on June 4, 2018. I approached my new role with curiosity and compassion. What did people find helpful? What was not helpful? How could we possibly reach so many people?

I began meeting individually with everyone who spent time working at the VSRC and as many people as possible who had any type of connection to the incident. I reached out to other resiliency centers and communities that had incidents of mass violence. I went on "ride alongs" and "sit alongs" with local law enforcement agencies, fire departments, and dispatch centers. Whenever I had the opportunity, I asked questions and did my best to listen and hear what was being said. I watched the conversations and posts on social media (with permission) to observe the many thoughts, feelings, and struggles of those in the online groups that had formed. I will never *know* the experience of anyone who was there or connected to someone who was there, but it was the beginning of my learning journey toward understanding what I needed to so that I could begin to help meet the behavioral health needs of those who did know.

I was given several projects that were already in progress to carry forward. Much planning had already begun, and the community was stepping up to offer support. I was also able to begin some projects. One such new project was the opportunity to produce a public service announcement (PSA). A representative from Nathan Adelson Hospice approached the VSRC with a request for ideas on how to use some grant funds. After visiting the center and exploring many options, hospice officials selected the PSA as a project. I requested and received the assistance of many of those with whom I had been in contact to serve on focus groups and help write the script. There was a lot of discussion about the language and terminology to be used, especially "1 October." Those creating the PSA insisted on using that term, and those affected by the incident insisted on *not* using it. That was not how they referred to it. It did not have meaning for them, and it diminished their experience. At one point, the producer told me that I had too many people participating in the PSA's production. However, I persisted with the belief that it was important to represent as many of the types of the affected individuals as possible, whether they spoke a phrase, a word, or no words.

The PSA turned out very well, has been widely shared and viewed, and is even used by the National Organization for Victim Assistance (NOVA) in its training. A sixty-second version (for social media) and a thirty-second version (for TV) were produced in both English and Spanish. No actors were used, only individuals connected to the incident.

The PSA and other experiences along the way have taught us that language and terminology matter. Many terms commonly used in connection to an incident of mass violence are not terms with which those affected want to be identified. It has been very important to accept all feedback and comments, especially the critical ones, to find effective and compassionate ways to communicate with the thousands of individuals that we hope to reach and support.

Every Journey Is Unique

Everyone has a unique path and timeline for healing that must be honored. Some people talked about how they connected with a professional right away and how much it helped. Many are still trying to figure out what type of help will be best for them.

I once took a panel of survivors to speak to a small group of students and faculty at the University of Nevada, Las Vegas. One of the comments from a panelist was that there are "twenty-two thousand ways" to cope and to heal. Each conversation with anyone connected to the incident is different and offers an opportunity to find both similarities in the experience and uniqueness.

In my work, I have spoken with several people who were at the concert together who later described entirely different observations about what they saw and heard. "Don't you remember all of the red cups?" "I don't remember any red cups, but I saw so many shoes and boots on the ground."

The concept of "readiness" shows up on a regular basis with those seeking support. After more than four years, survivors, family members, and others who were affected are reaching out for the first time. Some are reaching out with a need to re-engage in support or services as new world events and life experiences cause unexpected reactions.

Nontraditional Services

These conversations have also led to the discovery that many tools, strategies, and services can help heal the trauma of mass violence. The vsrc has attempted to respond to this by offering opportunities to explore information on a wide variety of topics and various experiential techniques. These have been offered both in person and virtually. Some examples include music therapy; art activities; trauma recovery yoga; mindfulness and meditation; peer support groups; individual peer support; psychoeducation on evidence-based therapeutic practices; goal and intention setting; creating vision boards; the effect of trauma on relationships; coping with grief and bereavement; and panel presentations from Route 91 Harvest Festival survivors and survivors of other incidents.

Peer Support

One of the things that I learned from listening and observing was that people were often turning to each other in the Route 91 Harvest Festival community for support before they were seeking formal services that were being offered. This sparked the idea that with some training and guidance, formal peer support could be very beneficial. I was able to connect with a nationally recognized expert to explore the idea. With Cherie Castellano's patience and guidance, HEART (Healing, Empowering And Rebuilding Together) was developed.

We engaged a lead coach who had been facilitating a virtual support group through the vsrc and a lead peer who was very active in the Route 91 Harvest Festival community. Each met Castellano's requirements to be a reciprocal peer support model.

The first training was completed in March 2021, and the program is now underway. Trained peer mentors who were affected in various ways by the incident offer individual support to others who were affected. Peer mentors are assigned clinical coaches for ongoing support and guidance. We believe the program is the first of its kind for this type of population. It is most often offered virtually, with mentors and peers throughout the United States, Canada, and Wales. Peer support is a unique type of support because it is a connection with someone else who was affected by the incident. Trained peer mentors guide the conversations. They are casual, yet genuine connections that can be created because they have a common lived experience.

THERAPY

While I do want to emphasize the value of peer support, it is important not to dismiss the value of the training and skills of an objective third party who can provide formal mental health services. The VSRC offers information so that those who have decided to seek therapy can be informed consumers about types of therapy, how to choose a therapist, and other related topics. One of the many challenges for the VSRC is that those affected live in such a wide geographical area. We will help anyone who contacts us, regardless of where they live, to find a qualified provider. We have reached out to providers in many states, Canada, and a few other countries. Those we contacted to ask about their qualifications and interest in working with those we serve sometimes didn't respond or responded "no." Others responded with generosity and gratefulness for the opportunity to help.

The immediate needs of those who experience a mass violence incident are different than those of people who have had time to realize that they might benefit from therapy. In the immediate aftermath of such a tragedy, typical formal therapeutic techniques are often not sought out and may not be the most beneficial approach. This does not mean that trained mental health professionals cannot be helpful at that time. However, it is important that they be trained in how to use their training, knowledge, and skills in a manner that applies to the situation. A traditional service agency or clinic may open its doors and welcome those affected. However, they may not be likely to find these open doors without the support and guidance of someone they trust. During that time, they are seeking safe spaces where they can gather, seek comfort, and continue to have hope.

THE WIDESPREAD IMPACT

Considering the large number of people involved and how widely they are dispersed throughout the country, the impact is incomprehensible. The Las Vegas community's support for those who were local was astounding. "Vegas Strong" was posted everywhere as a sign of this support. The perspectives on this phrase have been varied. Of course, the message of compassion and unity was important. But for some, the words were also a "trigger" or something that made it very difficult to move on. For a period of time, these kinds of messages were also shared nationally and worldwide. I attended a conference out of state later in October 2017. After a few of the breakout sessions, I began introducing myself as being from Nevada instead of Las Vegas. Otherwise, the conversation quickly turned to the shooting. While inquiries about the shooting were clearly well intentioned, they also took away my sense of choice. I did not want to talk about it with new people multiple times a day.

While the news was quite prominent and widespread for a while, many people also went home to communities distant from Las Vegas. These communities' responses varied. In some places, those around them did not seem to be aware of what had happened, or it was quickly set aside for more recent news. In some places, everyone knew and recognized them. Some were able to access the care they needed quickly, and some reported feeling very "alone," regardless of the community size, because they did not know anyone else there who had been at the festival.

We are also continuing to discover new groups of people who were affected by the mass shooting on the Las Vegas Strip. There are those individuals and groups that are easily recognized as "survivors," "victims," "responders," "medical providers," and so forth. However, there are also Good Samaritans; the resort community; reporters and those involved with media coverage; traffic camera operators; members of the Nevada Taxicab Authority who monitored admittance into the Family Assistance Center; those who collected and catalogued memorabilia; those who manage and maintain the Las Vegas Community Healing Garden; groups who identify with those affected; and many more. Just the estimated ticket holders and those who responded immediately totaled more than twenty-four thousand. We know that there are many more. It is important to remember that each of those directly affected also has family members, friends, neighbors, students, teachers, and others who care about them. The true number of those affected will not ever truly be known.

Collaborating

The majority of Route 91 Harvest Festival ticket holders were from California. As a result of this, many informal support programs were offered in the various communities to which they returned. Additionally, an

Antiterrorism and Emergency Assistance Program (AEAP) grant was offered to Ventura County to provide services in a way similar to the Vegas Strong Resiliency Center. Connecting with them regularly as they created their messaging and support services has been very valuable. Ventura's program did not have to start from scratch because we were able to share many lessons learned. We also have benefited from hearing new ideas and feedback that Ventura's team has gathered and shared.

REMEMBERING

It is very important to anyone connected to the tragedy to commemorate various annual events, such as loved ones' birthdays, holidays, and the date on which the shooting occurred. It is important to them to know that others remember and to not feel forgotten.

Each year on October 1, the incident is remembered, and the lives lost are honored in many ways. These ceremonial events and opportunities to gather and connect are important to each person for their own reasons. The types of events and the reactions of those involved change each year and will continue to do. The VSRC offers additional support and reaches out to those organizing events to offer the presence of the VSRC staff and emotional support volunteers.

October 1, 2018, was an amazing opportunity for me to meet face to face for the first time with many of the Route 91 Harvest Festival community with whom I had been in contact. They came to Las Vegas to commemorate the event, and I found myself listening to many stories of lives lost and lives saved, injuries and recovery (both physical and nonphysical), confusion over psychological symptoms experienced, and life events during the previous year. Our support was primarily offering information about available services and listening to their experiences. They appeared to appreciate the opportunity to reconnect with others while also feeling deep sadness, confusion, and loss. Some were able to describe healing and recovery. Some were visibly distraught. Most were somewhere in between.

Teams of therapy dogs were a source of support for many visitors and local groups, particularly first responders. We even responded to a request for dog teams to meet up with survivors in front of a casino on a Friday night. It was quite a scene: three therapy dog teams, the survivors, and many visitors at the casino entrance!

On October 1, 2019, I continued to meet new people, but I also had the opportunity to reconnect with people I had met or communicated with throughout the previous two years and hear about their journeys during that time. One individual in particular was very memorable for me. During the one-year commemoration, she had become distraught and shared her struggles with me. She was having no success finding someone to offer the type of services she needed where she lived. I gave her my information and hoped over the next few weeks that I would hear from her. When I did, I began the search for providers in her area and was honored to have had the opportunity to assist. I checked in a few times afterward to offer any additional assistance that she might need, but mostly received updates on the ups and downs of her healing journey. During a two-year commemoration event, a colleague told me that someone was looking for me and later, when I turned toward her, I had that moment of uncertainty about whether this was someone I had met before. Then I realized it was someone I had spent time with the previous year, but at that time it was through her tears. She looked so different to me this time because she was smiling! She let me know that she was still healing, but she was on her way and wanted to thank me for listening and helping her find what she needed for her journey. She introduced me to her companion. Reconnecting with her was an honor that I cannot describe.

In 2020, one of the most unusual and powerful events that I have had the honor to witness was called "Healing Ink." It was offered through Artists 4 Israel and was made possible entirely through donations. Tattoo artists from all over the country traveled to Las Vegas for the event. They were matched with those who were selected through an application process, and each pair worked together to create and apply a "scar that they chose." As with many events, the VSRC offered trained volunteers for emotional support for those receiving tattoos as well as the artists. Being present to hear about the significant meaning of each design and to watch as they were created was, once again, an honor beyond words. A few covered scars (that were *not* chosen) received as a result of the shooting. Many were symbols and representations of the experience, survival, loss, and commemoration. It was an intense experience, with artists and receivers forging new and lasting connections.

I also spent time at the Las Vegas Community Healing Garden and spoke with many who were visiting. I was able to talk with some and just "be there" with others. I met parents and other loved ones of the deceased, festival staff who wanted to honor the lives lost, and many who experienced their own grief and challenges from various connections and in various ways. I learned the meaning behind the many decorations on and around the trees. I also learned that people were still trying to understand how and why this happened. One young man was grieving the loss of his best friend. His parents were with him and talked about how difficult it has been to "not know what to do" to watch his experience of sadness and loss. One gentleman struggled to recognize the faces of those deceased; he was certain that he must have seen them while working there that night.

In 2021, there were more in-person events and more visitors. There were more smiles, but there were still those who seemed to be wandering and uncertain how to move on. I had the opportunity to witness the power of peer support in action. I was talking with someone at the Healing Garden whom I had met before, but I was still struggling to find successful strategies for healing. Our conversation was good, but his uncertainty was unresolved. I noticed a survivor I knew who entered the garden, and I had the opportunity to introduce them to each other. There was an immediate connection, and my presence was no longer noticed. I observed as he was introduced to others and was included in their group photo!

There was such a mixture of conversations at the four-year commemoration. More people were finding ways to move forward and heal than in prior years' events. It was inspiring to hear of their progress, their various paths for healing, and the strength found to continue their lives with meaning and connections. However, too many were still struggling, feeling the pain as if no time had passed, and looking for understanding and relief.

I often feel helpless. It is such an honor to have someone who has been through such a horrific event share any part of it with you. There is so much pain in the stories, and nothing can be offered to "undo" what has been done. No one will go back to being who they were before. They have so many questions. When will I be "over" this? When will it stop hurting? When will the memories of what I saw go away? I do not have the answers that they are seeking. I am only able to listen, offer a safe space for what they are going through, and gently engage in a conversation that will hopefully help that person on their own unique journey of healing and moving forward.

During recent years, I have received generous and complimentary feedback about how helpful I have been, sometimes just by being there and listening, and other times with specific actions and efforts to find what meets an individual's need, or in offering support to the overall community. The truth is that my interactions with those in the Route 91 Harvest Festival community are truly reciprocal in nature. When they are willing to share with me, I learn more and more about the needs and struggles of the community. This, in turn, helps me to figure out ways to be most helpful. I began to routinely let them know that, whether they will ever know the details, they are paying it forward, because someone else will benefit in the future from what I have been able to learn from them.

On my journey of learning and accompanying others on theirs for healing, I have learned:

- No two experiences of that night were the same.
- No two journeys of healing are the same.
- Healing is not a straight line or a linear experience.
- There are bumps, hills, valleys, turns, and plateaus.
- Understanding context and stages of healing is very important to providing services and support.
- An individual's needs will change over time.
- No one wants to feel forgotten or as if the incident no longer matters.
- We must listen first, ask questions, and then problem-solve together.
- While there is expertise and knowledge that helps us help others, the only "expert" on one person's experience and needs is that person.
- It is important to be open to new and different ideas about strategies and techniques for healing, but they must be based in trauma and applicable to those being served.
- Most people want to help when something so terrible happens.
- Most of those people are unsure about how to help.
- Commemoration of the event is very important.
- There are many ways to simply "be present," and sometimes that is all we can do.
- It is an honor and a gift to do so.

9

"I like safe noise."

Working with Survivors, Vegas Strong Resiliency Center

LAURIE LYTEL, Vegas Strong Resiliency Center volunteer therapist

On the morning of October 2, 2017, my cell phone lit up with messages and texts. Friends and family texted from across the globe. My college roommate called from Paris. My nephew from Washington, DC: "Aunt Laurie, are you OK?"

Why would he say that? I was puzzled. I glanced at my phone and caught the headline: "Las Vegas Shooting: 58 Killed and More Than 500 Hurt Near Mandalay Bay"[1]

It seemed unbelievable. Information was changing rapidly. I scrolled through Facebook posts, and I realized that many therapists were thinking the same thing: where can we go to help? Mental health professionals were meeting at Bridge Counseling Associates, a community nonprofit mental health agency that has been serving the Las Vegas community since 1971. I knew Bridge Counseling well; I worked there when I moved to Las Vegas in 1991.

I was scheduled to teach a class of soon-to-be-Master of Social Work students at the University of Nevada, Las Vegas, that afternoon. *It would probably be good to hold the class and talk with graduate social work students about helping in a crisis,* I thought. *No, it's best I go help in a crisis.* I canceled class for the day.

The shooting happened at 10:05 p.m. Sunday, October 1, 2017. About eight o'clock Monday morning, I started driving along West Charleston Boulevard toward the Bridge Counseling office.

Soon, I saw a massive gathering of people lining the street, snaking in and out of the parking lot. Hundreds of Las Vegans, seeking to help, drove to donate blood at United Blood Services. Cars and trucks pulled over on both sides, up and down the street. People circulated among the crowd to hand out coffee, orange juice, and snacks. Later, we learned there were more blood donations than could be used.

I arrived at Bridge Counseling amid many other volunteers. I was directed to Circus Circus, a hotel-casino a few miles north of Mandalay Bay on the Las Vegas Strip.

The parking lot in front of the casino was eerily empty. I passed the idle valet staff in their maroon uniforms, who were checking their phones nervously. I walked under the enormous pink and white neon canopy filled with hundreds of gold light bulbs and into the front lobby.

Casinos are never quiet. Electronic tones, whirring, repetitive beeps, pings, and jangly rings filled the air despite few customers. I wound my way past the oversize slot machines and found a cocktail waitress. I told her that I was a mental health volunteer and asked her how to get to the ballrooms.

"Thanks for coming," she said, as she leaned over and hugged me. She led me past the long craps tables, past the green-felt roulette table filled with black and red squares, through a maze of hallways, to the long escalator leading down to the ballroom. As I rode the escalator down, I saw uniformed hotel staff carrying water and coffee, security officers surveying the scene, and people gathering in the ballroom.

An array of mental health professionals showed up to volunteer: clinical social workers, marriage and family therapists, chemical dependency counselors, psychologists, school counselors, students, clinical interns, seasoned therapists, pastors.

Tourists visiting Las Vegas found their way to our ad-hoc command center. Two German women offered translation services. Many others offered their time and expertise: psychotherapists from California and New York; a retired psychiatrist from Maryland; an acupuncturist; massage therapists, and a traumatologist (an academic researcher who studied trauma).

People brought their therapy dogs. Mental health agencies deployed staff members throughout Las Vegas.

I have taught at UNLV for thirteen years and have been a licensed clinical social worker in Las Vegas for more than twenty-five years. I saw former colleagues from the Nevada Division of Child and Family Services. I recognized many of these volunteers, all offering their time. I felt proud to see so many UNLV students.

Round tables covered with white tablecloths filled the ballroom. It looked set for a dinner party. The hotel staff poured coffee and set baskets of snacks on each table. We wandered around, wanting to help, and feeling helpless. I saw two colleagues who fortunately brought their laptops. We realized we had to organize ourselves.

After a brief huddle, we decided that we needed a list of everyone milling around. We asked people for copies of their credentials, and everyone started pulling up their licenses on their phones. A long line formed in front of us as we built our list of emergency mental health professionals.

A manager from Bridge Counseling was in contact with the Las Vegas Convention Center, which became the city's emergency command center. We received requests for mental health support at different businesses and casinos, and we dispatched counselors to various sites throughout the day.

While we sought to offer mental health services, there were many more acute needs. Unbeknown to us at the time, medical personnel were still struggling to identify bodies. Family members were flying to Las Vegas. Relatives were frantically searching the hospitals, funeral homes, and the coroner's office to locate their loved ones. The concert site had been shut down, so no one could retrieve their wallets or phones.

On October 2, 2017, there were more mental health volunteers than we had places to send them. But we all knew the emotional devastation that lay ahead.

Coping with the Traumatic Aftermath

Many schools and workplaces have adopted trauma-informed approaches. Since the Route 91 Harvest Festival shooting, Las Vegas hotel-casinos have an increased awareness of potential trauma responses as well. I live in the northwest part of Las Vegas, close to Red Rock Casino Resort. Its officials seem aware of the potential disruption fireworks might cause for residents. Since October 1, 2017, the resort mails letters to nearby residents before the Fourth of July, New Year's Eve, and other occasions when fireworks occur:

> Dear Neighbor,
> On . . . , a special event will take place at Red Rock Casino. This event will feature a fireworks display, and due to your close proximity to Red Rock, we would like to make you aware of the event.
> The fireworks . . . will last approximately 10 minutes. We hope you

will enjoy the fireworks display as much as we are looking forward to celebrating the holiday with the community. . . .

Thank you for your cooperation.

Responses vary to the same shared traumatic experience. Like watching a car crash at a busy intersection from four different corners, each observer experiences the trauma through their eyes. Thousands attended that third night of the Route 91 Harvest Festival. Some festivalgoers were directly in the line of fire, others stood in front of the stage, and even more were spread out around the fifteen-acre venue. Some were near an exit; most were not. Everyone's location during the shooting invariably shaped their experiences.

Many pieces shape a person's response to trauma: their own childhoods, personal experiences, friends, family, and social support. Family history and genetics also shape a person's response to trauma. A preexisting mental health issue, such as anxiety and/or depression, may intensify in the aftermath of a traumatic event. Someone with a history of abuse, neglect, or trauma sometimes lives with an internal narrative: *Here it is. It's happening again.*

During a trauma, the brain goes into survival mode and overrides normal cognitions. Often, everything seems slower and brighter and louder. Over time, these images from the event can become triggers. Triggers are reminders of a traumatic event, which can feel relentless: smells, sounds, sights. Parks, open spaces, concerts, flashing lights, police cars, loud noises, ambulances, sirens. Even memories of the weather that day can evoke feelings for survivors. For many Route 91 Harvest Festival ticket holders, country music continues to trigger memories of the shooting.

One festival attendee, Ajay Ritter, told me, "I like safe noise." She worked to desensitize herself, explaining, "I followed ambulances for a while. It helped that I was behind them. I did that until the flashing lights didn't freak me out anymore."[2]

When the shooting started, many people thought they heard fireworks. The shooter was devastating in his initial ability to hide the noise of the massacre. Fireworks continue to be a powerful trigger for many.

Another source of sensitized public response comes from the Vegas Golden Knights, the NHL franchise that began its inaugural season the same month as the mass shooting. The Golden Knights rose to the challenge of this trauma, helping the community in numerous ways. A trauma-informed awareness is present at each game.[3]

Pregame festivities at the Golden Knights games mimic Las Vegas shows, often with flashing lights, flares, and strobes. Before any pyrotechnics, a warning comes across the massive video board in T-Mobile Arena: "Effects warning. Haze, lasers, and strobe effects will be used during tonight's game." And sometimes, "Hey, relax, we meant to do this."

A warning such as this doesn't protect survivors from having an emotional response, but they might feel less caught off guard. And perhaps after some time, they can feel unsettled rather than terrified.

Many survivors wrestle with fragmented memories. Many experience recurring flashing images, such as walking over injured or dead people to save themselves or being unable to help the person nearby. Several survivors told me that their spouses shielded them, literally taking the bullet.

Our brains create many different emotional responses in efforts to make sense of an unimaginable traumatic event. It can be helpful to imagine some of these responses on a continuum: dissociation, flashbacks, memories. When a person dissociates, they feel disconnected from those around them, out of touch with reality, sometimes as if they are floating. Dissociation involves losing track of the moment in time and place.

Flashbacks can also feel dissociative, but a flashback recalls a specific traumatic memory, when someone feels as if they are reliving that moment in time, as if the trauma is happening at that moment, again.

A memory, however, not a flashback or dissociation, allows someone to remain present in time and place. That person remains in contact with people around them. A memory usually includes continuity, while a flashback feels like a jolt.

After the initial shock, new challenges face trauma survivors: integrating the memories into their own life narratives. It is a process of placing the trauma into one's life story, accepting it as part of a personal history. This process often takes many years.

Over time, when a person can integrate traumatic memories, the feeling of shock softens, and the event feels less immediate. Progress toward healing occurs when a survivor can recall the event, remain present in place and time, and retain a sense of calm during those memories.

The memories will always be present, but the hope is that the impact softens over time. The struggle is to make a kind of peace with the memories.

Some survivors mistakenly believe that if they just "forget" the event, they will be okay. But years of trauma research has confirmed otherwise. Many trauma survivors voice similar hopes: *Get over it. Get back to my regular life. Forget about it. Move on.*

Trauma leaves permanent imprints for virtually everyone. A person's sense of time is often altered. The world looks different than before. A single solid line divides time: before and after.

Over a lifetime, most people experience some trauma in their lives. Trauma can evoke a wide range of responses, at times resulting in post-traumatic stress disorder (PTSD). Most people who experience trauma do not develop PTSD. Research suggests that 4–12 percent of people who experience trauma will develop PTSD. Certain kinds of trauma, such as sexual assault and mass shootings, result in higher rates of PTSD. People involved in a mass shooting have an estimated 28 percent chance of developing PTSD.[4]

There are many aspects of long-term recovery from trauma. A critical component is accepting the realization that a person's belief system feels cracked or broken, unalterably changed.

This realization, which sometimes takes years to accept, is often experienced as a profound loss. Route 91 Harvest Festival survivors report that they lost a sense of safety, freedom of movement to enjoy concerts, feel carefree, be outside, live in the moment. These losses can last a lifetime. Many trauma survivors struggle mightily to regain a sense of safety in the world.

Research identifies aspects that help trauma survivors cope: robust social and family support and a strong sense of spirituality or religion. People who live with someone tend to heal better from trauma than people who live alone.[5]

If the event is a shared experience, trauma survivors often cope better in the aftermath. This has been the case after earthquakes, tsunamis, and the attack on the World Trade Center on September 11, 2001. In contrast, when someone experiences a personal trauma (such as sexual assault), they often lack external validation about the trauma. This isolation can compound a survivor's struggles.

After a mass shooting, there is often a cohesive group of survivors who band together. They knew each other before and after the shooting, and in that respect, are a built-in support system. This was true for several mass shootings: Columbine High School (1999) in Littleton, Colorado; Sandy Hook Elementary School (2012) in Newtown, Connecticut; Stoneman Douglas High School (2018) in Parkland, Florida; and Pulse nightclub (2016) in Orlando, Florida.

In 2017, at the Route 91 Harvest Festival, there were no natural groups in the immediate aftermath. There were twenty-two thousand ticket holders, and they came from all over the world. There were groups of friends who attended the concert together, but there was no larger connected community.

An annual ritual, the Sunrise Remembrance Ceremony, outside the Clark County Government Center, draws survivors, politicians, and first responders, standing together to remember those lost. This way of honoring survivors and remembering trauma in a group supports many in their grieving. People are less alone, less isolated.

Out of this trauma emerged the Vegas Strong Resiliency Center (VSRC), "a place of healing and support dedicated to serving as a multi-agency resource and referral center for residents, visitors, and responders affected by the shooting at Route 91 Harvest Festival." The center, managed by the Legal Aid Center of Southern Nevada, helps people access resources to help them build strength and resiliency.[6]

The VSRC also provides referrals for mental health services. Support groups began almost immediately, and they moved online through the COVID-19 pandemic. Vegas Strong groups are in several places across the US and Canada.

Many other Vegas Strong events have been organized specifically for those who attended the concert. Every event has mental health professionals present. I attended a survivor-only reunion in 2019 as a mental health volunteer. Many people wore T-shirts proclaiming their identities. Among the variety of messages: Route 91 Strong; *You Can't Help Me. I Want My Daughter Back*; Country Strong; 58 Empty Barstools; Forever Family Strong; Addicted to the Twang; Route 91 Family; Whiskey Helps; Alcohol Amplified Tour; Fuck PTSD; Fuck That Guy.

One man told me: "I'm a New Yorker, and I was at 9/11. It's been 18 years now, and I can still smell it." A father told me how he ran around the aftermath of the site, lifting the shirts of people lying on the ground, searching for his daughter's tattoo.

I met a butler from Mandalay Bay. He insisted: "If that was my floor,

I would have checked on it. I could have stopped that guy." Many people struggle to make sense of the trauma on their own.

There are many avenues for recovery from traumatic events. The trauma field has expanded significantly in the last several years. Many therapies specifically focus on trauma, and many more therapies offer multiple treatment approaches. Sometimes people can work through their trauma with family, friends, and faith leaders. Others find that their friends and family cannot bear to listen.

There are well-accepted therapies that are often used to treat trauma: trauma-focused cognitive-behavioral therapy; eye movement desensitization and reprocessing; cognitive processing therapy; and prolonged exposure therapy. Many people need psychoeducation about the long-term nature of trauma recovery and PTSD.

Many additional kinds of treatment prove helpful as well: somatic therapy; polyvagal therapy; dialectical behavioral therapy; emotionally focused therapy; and acceptance and commitment therapy. Many people also find alternate approaches useful: therapy dogs, equine therapy, animal-assisted interventions, prayer groups, drum circles, art therapy, and trauma recovery yoga.

Another example of an alternative approach is Healing Ink, a project of the nonprofit group Artists 4 Israel, which helps survivors of violence heal through the art of tattooing. In 2020, tattoo artists from all over the country came to Las Vegas to offer tattoos for those affected by the Route 91 Harvest Festival shooting.[7] As the organization explains: "Healing Ink is the only organization in the world pledged to utilizing the power of tattoos to ease the physical and emotional pain caused by war and terrorism...survivors...of terrorism report tremendous healing and strengthening. . . . We believe that scars are sometimes a painful reminder and that the only way to ease that pain is to create another, more powerful mark on the body."[8]

One woman who was at the festival asked me: "Where were they—the police, the medical personnel? We waited for hours for them to show up." It is an artifact of trauma that time becomes distorted. What may have been five minutes may have felt like an hour.

Many Las Vegas residents and festival attendees were critical of the emergency response. Anger, resentment, and harsh accusations were leveled against government officials; the Las Vegas Metropolitan Police Department; the sheriff; and MGM Resorts International (owners of

Mandalay Bay and the site on which the festival was held) executives, employees, and maids. As if they should have known, as if they should have been able to stop the unthinkable tragedy.

Monday morning quarterbacking often seems brilliant. After September 11, 2001, and 1 October 2017, questions arose: how could we not be prepared? We were not and could not be prepared because these violent tragedies were outside the bounds of our collective imaginations.

Many criticisms are born of grief. For most human beings, it is less painful and less lonely to blame hotel staff, police, medical and fire personnel than to face the heartbreaking truth: my loved one is gone, and no one can save us from this pain.

Unlocking the Gates—Spontaneous Healing

On October 1, 2021, new kinds of healing emerged. That year, I decided to join the human chain, an anniversary ritual that started in 2018, forming a huge circle around the Route 91 Harvest Festival venue. The site had been closed off by chain-link fencing since 2017.

We gathered early outside the fence. We lined up directly across from the concert venue, at the intersection of Giles Street and East Ali Baba Lane. East Reno Avenue bordered the north side of the site, Las Vegas Boulevard South (the Strip) the west, and Mandalay Bay Road the south. Police cars blocked off the entire street, enabling people to move around safely.

I glanced across the street and saw the huge jet fuel tanks at McCarran (now Harry Reid) International Airport. Apparently, the shooter tried to pierce the gas tanks, but they were full of kerosene and did not explode.

Two women, wearing their orange and black Route 91 Harvest Festival T-shirts, distributed flashing neon bracelets. The bracelets must be cracked and shaken to activate the neon liquid. Then there are wrist fasteners to latch.

But I couldn't do this one-handed. I knew no one around me, but we were all there for the same reason. I asked the man next to me, "Hey there, could you help me out with this?"

He easily fastened my bracelet, which then glowed lavender. His was yellow, while his wife's bracelet radiated bright orange.

I thanked him, and we started talking. They lived in Long Beach, California, and decided to return to Las Vegas for the fourth-year anniversary events. After they returned home in 2017, they both struggled to regain a sense of stability. For months after the shooting, when sirens wailed in their neighborhood, his wife fell to the floor to find safety. Seeking to address her hyperreactivity, she located a trauma therapist who helped her through eye movement desensitization and reprocessing (EMDR) therapy.

The lights of Mandalay Bay, Delano Las Vegas, and the Luxor lit up the concert venue in 2017. In 2021, the concert site became a parking lot for events at Allegiant Stadium, which houses the Las Vegas Raiders and UNLV football. MGM Resorts International has announced plans to turn the site into a community and athletic center.

MGM Resorts also donated two acres in the northeast part of the site for a permanent 1 October memorial. A memorial committee continues to develop the details. Despite this, many survivors wish the entire site was a memorial.

In 2021, as we rounded the corner toward the Strip, the gold-colored Mandalay Bay loomed directly in front of us. Ritter pointed up at the towering hotel, showing me where the shooter had barricaded himself. We walked slowly with the crowd around the entire venue, and as we neared our starting point, we heard an eruption of voices.

"They're letting us in!" echoed along the dark street, lit up by flashing police vehicles lining the street. MGM Resorts officials had decided to let survivors back into the site, something people had been requesting for four years.

Just inside the chain-link fence, representatives from MGM Resorts, the Las Vegas Metropolitan Police Department, and the Vegas Strong Resiliency Center stood silently. I suspected we all felt the same apprehension. People walked in slowly, gingerly, in groups, holding hands, hugging one another. They ventured to different parts of the parking lot.

Clusters of people in twos or threes walked onto the site, moving slowly with their arms around one another. It was quiet. Surrounded by the lights of the Las Vegas Strip, the venue was brightly lit at 11 p.m.

Relatives and friends knew where their loved ones had fallen; it seemed they returned to these areas.

Some families sat in circles holding hands. One man kneeled on one knee as his head bent in prayer.

About ten feet away, another man kneeled on both knees, praying.

One man sat down with his legs stretched straight out in front of him. He was taking swigs from a bottle wrapped in a brown bag.

Some lay flowers down where their loved one's last living moments had occurred. The bereaved sat facing the same way, where the stage was, on the south end of the property. Many wore cowboy hats and boots.

The air was filled: crying, wailing, singing, radios playing country music. Some were playing Jason Aldean's song "When She Says Baby," which he was singing when the shooting started.

It was an unplanned, profound healing experience for many. A mostly empty lot, with survivors huddled throughout. Somehow, on this night, four years later, this site felt safe. A chain-link fence, and in some spots double fencing, surrounded it. The flashing lights of police cars parked outside the venue offered a sense of protection.

Loved ones knew what they needed to do to heal. There was no announcement in advance, but they had been waiting for this moment for four years. As a therapist, I realized later that they did this without any professional or therapeutic intervention. Later, many posts on Facebook[9] underscored this:

Ritter commented:

Last night was amazing. Finally, after four years, MGM [Resorts officials] let everyone walk the site. They let us all come in the venue grounds for the first time since the night of October 1, 2017. We felt a weight lifted off of us after we left. Lots of closure and healing going on! Hoping with that, my mind has had some closure.

Shannon Caffey explained:

We and many other survivors and families got to go inside the Route 91 [Harvest Festival] venue last night. . . . We walked and talked about our escape route and what happened that night. Being there was so surreal, and we couldn't believe they let us in. But it happened finally, and as we were leaving, we felt like something heavy was lifted off of us. We felt more closure and more healing as many others did also. We were so blessed to be there last night to get to do this. We pray that they will give access to many others that want to go in there and find closure and more healing soon.

Christina J. Oleson wrote:

Four years ago, our lives were nearly taken in an act of great evil. Though [we were] injured, our lives were spared. Two ankle replacements, two knee surgeries, almost four years of physical therapy, and countless X-rays, MRIs, and doctor appointments. And yet, the recovery remains ongoing to this day. There are good days and worse, but this year the memory of that night seems to weigh more heavily on our souls. Still, we know that this too will pass. We cried out to God that night while we laid on the ground praying. And He heard us.

Nadine Lusmoeller commented:

Celebrate life today as well. Let's be grateful that we're still here to see the sun rise, to breathe the fresh air, to feel it on our skin. Celebrate the people we've met, the friends we've made and what we've learned. When you go through trauma and hard times, it often becomes difficult to see past the pain. Healing from trauma is tough. Healing from trauma isn't easy . . . there is no shortcut for healing. We will never be able to forget that horrific night four years ago, but we can learn to live with it. Don't let the memories slow you down. There is hope—for all of us. Fight because the world needs you. It needs someone who's been strengthened by adversity and struggle. It needs you, who have been through so much but still manage to remain kind and compassionate. When everything seems dark, choose to be the light.

NOTES

1. Andrew Blankstein et al., "Las Vegas Shooting: 58 Killed and More Than 500 Hurt Near Mandalay Bay." Retrieved October 1, 2017, from https://www.nbcnews.com/storyline/las-vegas-shooting/las-vegas-police-investigating-shooting-mandalay-bay-n806461.

2. All the concert attendees quoted in this chapter have given their permission to use their full names.

3. Steve Carp, "October 1: How the Golden Knights Helped Las Vegas Heal." Retrieved October 1, 2021, from https://vegashockeynow.com/2021/10/01/october-1-how-the-golden-knights-helped-las-vegas-heal/.

4. Amy Novotney, "What Happens to the Survivors." In *American Psychological Association,* September 2018, vol. 49, no. 8.

5. Jamie L. Gradus, "Epidemiology of PTSD." US Department of Veterans Affairs. Retrieved February 23, 2016, from http://www.ptsd.va.gov/professional/PTSD-overview/.

6. Vegas Strong Resiliency Center. Accessed September 1, 2019. https://www
.vegasstrongrc.org/.

7. Brianna Erickson, "Healing Ink Event Helps Oct. 1 Survivors Write New Stories," in
Las Vegas Review-Journal, September 30, 2020.

8. Healing Ink. Accessed June 24, 2022. https://www.healingink.org/.

9. All those quoted approved their names and Facebook posts being included herein.

10

Dealing with Death

New Models for Grieving Are Emerging

Daniel Bubb, Associate Professor in Residence, UNLV Honors College

No one will forget the shocking and devastating images of the shooter firing thousands of bullets at twenty-two thousand people attending the Route 91 Harvest Festival. Terror and chaos permeated the site as panicked festivalgoers scrambled to get away. People hid in buildings, and some even breached the fence onto the grounds of McCarran (now Harry Reid) International Airport, prompting air traffic controllers to divert incoming flights to alternate airports. Local and national media began showing the chaos on television screens, provoking distressed phone calls and text messages from family members and friends to those attending the concert. Battalions of law enforcement officers swarmed Mandalay Bay to stop the shooter from continuing his gunfire. He ultimately took his own life. Hospital emergency rooms overflowed with shooting victims, and some hotels such as the Holiday Inn Express Las Vegas created makeshift emergency rooms in their lobbies to treat the wounded. At the site, fifty-eight people lost their lives, and almost nine hundred were injured in the worst mass shooting event in modern United States history (two people later died, bringing the death toll to sixty).[1] To this day, family members, friends, and strangers mourn those who lost their lives. All of this raises the obvious question of why the shooter opened fire on concert attendees. It also raises the question of how people still struggle to cope with the reality that sixty people are dead from this senseless and horrific event.

Everyone copes with death differently. Some people express their grief more openly; others are more private. Some people get over their grief in a relatively short amount of time; others take longer or do not get over grieving at all. Regardless of how people grieve over the death of loved ones or friends, no manual explains how to grieve and for how long. No instructions or training sessions explain how people are supposed to deal with death or handle the affairs of the deceased. The entire end-of-life process can be enormously stressful for both the person who is dying and the caretaker. To make matters worse, the situation becomes even more difficult when a mass shooting takes place and death is sudden and violent. Relatives and friends of the victims endure a spectrum of very powerful emotions ranging from shock and despair to deep depression. Even strangers to the victims feel the necessity of visiting makeshift memorial sites to leave flowers, a stuffed animal, a card, or some memento to convey their condolences, and to spiritually connect with the deceased. Such was the case with the horrendous October 1, 2017, mass shooting that traumatized family members and friends of the victims, and other Las Vegas valley residents. To commemorate the people who lost their lives, volunteers created a temporary memorial, the Las Vegas Community Healing Garden, to enable residents and out-of-town visitors to pay their respects.[2]

This chapter will explore how people express their grief about those who lose their lives in traumatic events such as mass shootings, and specifically how they communicate that grief in different forms. It will include models by prominent psychologists who explain the different ways that people grieve beyond the ubiquitously known Kübler-Ross model. Lastly, it specifically will relate those methods of communication and commemoration to the mass shooting in Las Vegas that continues to mentally and emotionally scar those who witnessed the event; knew someone who was either killed or physically injured; or were not there and did not know any of the victims but felt the necessity of expressing their condolences and grief to the victims and their families.

For anyone, coping with death is a very stressful, traumatic, and exhausting process. They are faced with the immediacy of making funeral arrangements, handling the affairs of the deceased, and having to move on with their lives. Thus, psychologists who have studied how people cope with death came up with a model that explains the different emotions and sequence of emotions through which survivors of the deceased endure. Elisabeth Kübler-Ross's model consists of five stages of emotions through which loved ones of the deceased go.[3] The first is refusal to accept the reality that the sick or injured person died. The survivor desperately searches for answers why their partner or friend has passed away. The next emotion is anger that the partner or friend has died. As part of the desperate search for answers, the survivor becomes angry that something different could have been done, or that not enough was done to keep the person from dying. The survivor feels that their partner or friend gave up the fight. The third emotion is bargaining when the survivor is desperate to keep their sick or injured partner alive by changing the way they live their life. For example, they might try to bargain with a religious deity to keep their partner or friend alive. The fourth stage is depression. The survivor falls into deep depression over that fact that their partner or friend has died. Life has become completely empty and lost purpose and meaning now that the deceased has been buried or cremated. Finally, the survivor has accepted the fact that their loved one has died and physically is gone forever. Many believe their memory will live on, but their body no longer is present.[4]

Despite the Kübler-Ross model's existence for decades, psychologists such as J. William Worden are questioning it as dated and not entirely accurate. They claim the Kübler-Ross model suggests finality with each stage when actually the stages occur at the same time and constantly remain in motion.[5] While Kübler-Ross has been widely used to analyze the phases of grief that people experience and endure, it suggests passive progression when reality suggests that all stages are ongoing. Each phase is not isolated with a specific termination date. The phases are interconnected and continuous. In a sense, the model connotes a sense of closure when there might not be any.

Psychologists such as Richard Kalish agree with the Kübler-Ross model that the emotions and related effects are the same in that survivors of the deceased experience those stages of grief.[6] However, there is more to those stages that are just as powerful. For example, psychologist Jane Littlewood claims there is shock, numbness, disbelief, anxiety, sadness, and relief.[7] She asserts that some people fall into meaninglessness, despair, loneliness, and confusion.[8] They might blame themselves, have guilt, and socially withdraw.

For some people, the grieving process is relatively brief, whereas for others, it can be extensive, perhaps even endless. Regardless, people search for some meaning about why a loved one or close friend died, and what could have been done differently to prevent the person's death. Additionally, to remember the deceased, at least temporarily, the survivor might create a makeshift shrine until proper burial can be done.[9]

In the case of mass shooting victims, makeshift shrines often are made to commemorate those who lost their lives. This is not only for relatives or friends of those who lost their lives, but for visitors who did not know the victims of the shooting. They desire to express their deep sadness, empathy, and anger. The shrines serve as vehicles for spiritual connectivity with the deceased. In addition to shrines, relatives and friends of the deceased might visit familiar places where fond memories were made. Essentially, by commemorating loved ones, survivors can begin the slow healing process.[10]

People commemorate loved ones or friends who die in many ways. Ceremonially, religious leaders will conduct the funeral, eulogizing the deceased. They administer funerary rituals such as offering prayer, and they invite family members and friends of the deceased to express words of remembrance. At the cemetery, monuments, headstones, and markers commemorate the deceased. Additionally, family members and friends place flowers on the gravesite or cremation niche as a spiritual remembrance.

In the case of mass shootings, to remember the victims who died, candlelight vigils often are held as a ceremony of mourning, remembrance, and peace. Also, moments of silence take place at sporting events. For instance, to commemorate the fifty-eight people who died at the site of the mass shooting, the NHL's Vegas Golden Knights held a moment of silence before their first home game just days later and retired a jersey with the number 58 on it.[11] The powerful symbolism was extraordinary. In another show of support for the victims, Illinois resident Greg Zanis was so distraught by what he saw that he took it upon himself to make crosses remembering those who lost their lives.[12]

Psychologists are providing a new model for grieving that provides guidance. Stephen A. Diamond argues that there is dread affiliated with the presumed nothingness that comes with death.[13] Life can feel empty, meaningless, and pointless when a loved one dies. There is anxiety of loss, fear, and disdain of death. Instead, Diamond claims that we should follow philosopher Carl Jung, who claimed death should be considered a meaningful destination in life.[14] While death is morbid to think about, it should be viewed as the end of the journey, celebrating the achievement of living life.[15] Despite the different models offered by psychologists, the fact remains that communicating one's grief also is an intrinsic part of the process to cope with the death of a loved one.

Historically, there were myriad ways through which people communicated the death of a loved one. The most common one that still exists today is an obituary in a newspaper. Obituaries often contain loving messages remembering the deceased. Additionally, the obituary will include a listing of relatives of the deceased and a location and time when a memorial service will take place. Some people will post a message on social media such as Facebook, Instagram, or Twitter, although this is uncommon because to many people, death is private, and announcing a loved one's death or remembering them might be strictly for immediate family members until the survivors are comfortable informing other people. Even then, survivors of the deceased still might prefer to not post anything on social media. At the same time, for those who are unable to attend the funeral, social media enables them to write a private, personal note to the survivors.

If the deceased is a victim of an event such as a mass shooting, people will post messages on the makeshift shrine or online through a professional memorial website to commemorate or celebrate the life of the deceased.[16] This is part of a spiritual process that gives visitors a sense of connection to the deceased, empathizing with the survivor, and trying to bring some sense of human understanding and compassion to what happened. According to scholar Jack Santino, as part of commemoration and performativity, people feel they need to witness the shrine at the place of the event to grieve, mourn, reflect, and connect with the deceased.[17]

Regardless of the way death is communicated, the memories of the mass shooting in Las Vegas remain just as painful to survivors of the deceased as the day of the tragedy. On October 1, 2019, at a gathering of family and friends of the victims, Joe Robbins, whose twenty-year-old son, Quinton, was killed in the shooting, asked, "What does one do with loss? What does one do with the grief?"[18] At the same ceremony, Frank Gibase announced he lost one of his best friends, Cameron Robinson, in the shooting.[19] Gibase claimed that grief taught him many things about life, the most important of which is to "appreciate life and cherish those around you." He added, "You never know what is going to happen." Before he left the gathering, Gibase wrote "[Cameron] You are always with us. We love you," on the white cross remembering his friend.[20]

Two years later, at another gathering commemorating those who lost their lives in the October 1, 2017, mass shooting, Dee Ann Hyatt, a concert attendee who was injured and survived, emotionally expressed that "I was wounded. Those physical wounds have healed. But the lasting scars for our family remain."[21] Hyatt lost her brother, Kurt von Tillow, a truck driver from northern California, in the mass shooting. She said, "We continue to live the impact of all that happened that night four years later. People thrive and people struggle to live with the physical and mental pain, and our lives are forever changed."[22]

To support the community, MGM Resorts International donated two acres of land on the Las Vegas Strip as a memorial space where visitors can mourn, reflect, and remember those who lost their lives. Tennille Pereira, director of the Vegas Strong Resiliency Center, said, "We still remember, we still respect, we still honor [those who lost their lives]. But it's not raw like it was and jarring. It just feels more hopeful and peaceful."[23] As a place for mourning, reflection, and remembrance of those who lost their lives, the space will help visitors spiritually heal, and deal with death.

Notes

1. Andrew Blankstein, Pete Williams, Rachel Elbaum, and Elizabeth Chuck, "Las Vegas Shooting: 59 Killed and More Than 500 Hurt Near Mandalay Bay," *NBC News,* October 2, 2017, nbcnews.com.

2. Regina Garcia Cano, "Garden Provides Place to Mourn Las Vegas Shooting Victims," *Associated Press,* September 29, 2018, apnews.com.

3. Richard A. Kalish, *Death, Grief, and Caring Relationships,* 2nd ed. (Monterey, CA: Brooks/Cole Publishing Company, 1985), 132–33.

4. Kalish, 132–133.

5. Daniel Bates, "The Four Tasks of Grieving," *Psychology Today,* November 8, 2019.

6. Kalish, *Death, Grief, and Caring Relationships 2nd Edition,* 132.

7. Jane Littlewood, *Aspects of Grief: Bereavement in Adult Life* (New York and London: Tavistock/Routledge Press, 1992), 42–43.

8. Littlewood, 44.

9. Littlewood, 44.

10. Jack Santino, ed., *Spontaneous Shrines and the Public Memorialization* (New York: Palgrave Publishers, 2006), 9.

11. Amir Vera, "Las Vegas Hockey Team Retires No. 58 to Honor Concert Victims," *CNN,* April 1, 2018, cnn.com.

12. Meredith Deliso, "Greg Zanis, Who Built Crosses to Honor Victims of Mass Shooting, Has Died," *ABC News,* May 4, 2020, abcnews.go.com.

13. Stephen A. Diamond, "Dealing with Death Anxiety: Part 2," *Psychology Today,* April 22, 2020, https://www.psychologytoday.com/us/blog/evil-deeds/202004/dealing-death-anxiety-0.

14. Diamond.

15. Diamond.

16. Tony Walter, "New Mourners, Old Mourners: Online Memorial Culture as a Chapter in the History of Mourning," *Review of Hypermedia and Multimedia* 21 (December 2014), 10.

17. Santino, *Spontaneous Shrines and Public Memorialization,* 9.

18. Ed Komenda, "'You're Always with Us': Two Years After Las Vegas Shooting, Community Navigates Loss," *Reno Gazette-Journal,* October 1, 2019, usatoday.com.

19. Komenda.

20. Komenda.

21. Ken Ritter, "Fourth Year Since Las Vegas Massacre: 'Be There for Each Other,'" *Associated Press,* September 30, 2021, lasvegassun.com.

22. Ritter.

23. Ritter.

11

"O word, thou word, that I lack—"

The Place of Poetic Mysticism in the Expression of Grief,
Or How Language Succeeds in Failing Us

ERYN GREEN, Assistant Professor in Residence, UNLV Department of English.
The author thanks historian Greg Hise, who kindly reviewed this article.

When I was asked by the president of the University of Nevada, Las Vegas, to write a poem commemorating the October 1, 2017, shooting in Las Vegas—where I live, work, teach, and raise my daughter with my wife, Hanna; which is to say, my whole world—I remember exactly the sensation ✳
✳ ✳ ✳ ✳ ✳ ✳ ✳ ✳ ✳ ✳   :

Breath catching throat. A desire and total inability to speak. I wanted to say yes, of course and simultaneously no, how could I—could anyone. It was an inarticulable feeling, an experience of paradox, almost to a stunned neuron, like that I felt waking up to the news of what had happened on the first day of October in 2017—how could anyone. It wasn't that I didn't know what I wanted to say. It was that I knew there was simply no way. Over the next month, I wrote a poem—"58 Bells"—which may have been the most difficult creative project I have ever—. Every word was wrong. Every line broke gracelessly. I failed and failed and failed.

✳ ✳ ✳ ✳ ✳ ✳ ✳

✳ ✳

When the time came to read, I talked about Arnold Schoenberg, who was not there, and could not hear me, and his unfinished masterpiece, *Moses and Aaron,* and the famous line where—reckoning the presence of God, suffering, indifference, sublimity, and responsibility—Moses, tasked with translating an eternal system of communication, far beyond human ears, is finally overtaken, and falls to his knees:

> *"O word, thou word, that I lack!"*

The more I think about the tragedy we're addressing here today, the more that cry—and the moments, the minutes, the hours that occasioned it—stays with me.

> ∗

This is not a new idea.

In fact, as far as language is concerned, it might be one of the very oldest. Ancient poetic/mystic traditions have long understood language as a tool for approaching, but ultimately not fully countenancing, the ineffable—a means by which a kind of contact between we fragile few here on earth and those things beyond us might be made. The early poets of Kabbalah were interested, that's for sure:

> A measure of holiness,
> a measure of power,
> a measure of awe,
> a measure of trembling
> a measure of dread,
> a measure of anguish
> a measure of horror—
> a measure of the robe.[1]

begins one unattributable early poem of the Jewish Heikhalot/Merkavah mystic traditions (early Judaic "Poems of the Palace and Poems of the Chariot"). Words point at, yolk in, and invoke the ineffable, but they do not manage to fully convey the thing they attempt to contact, not entirely—hence the refrain, the revision, the ongoing vanishing point of description. Hence the next line (measure), and the next, and the next. The need for that ongoing.

∗   ∗

How can I say that these thoughts buoyed me in the days and weeks after the shooting? I remember going to teach class the next day we were allowed to do so, because, I thought, *What if anyone shows up? What if anyone doesn't?* How they buoy me—

*   *   *

I remember that I talked about doors that day. I've lost the syntax—*holding them open longer for strangers.* And looking one another in the eye. I failed and failed and failed. However, the failure—of my comportment in that moment, of language in the face of the unspeakable, of tongues and words and that which cannot be said—isn't lamentable—or not only—but rather, unexpectedly: although words fail to provide what they promise, it's maybe the case that what they teach in failing spurs us to better speaking being—is that possible? *How could—*

*   *   *   *

Of this instant at the end of Act 2 in Schoenberg's opera—which is, as David Jasper points out, "the musical end" of the work, "language is defeated by the very infinity which it reveals."[2]

Among the many historical uses of poetry is the attempted articulation of things that cannot be entirely said: the experience and awareness of love, joy, death, and loss. That no poem has ever fully succeeded in articulating these phenomena is not the point; or, rather, it is not the point, but not how we usually imagine. What I mean is, poems fail. Words fail. We fail—and most often, in the moments when the most incredible things catastrophically transpire. They, and we, fail to do the job we ostensibly assign ourselves—represent that which we experience. And yet we that remain, remain to try again, and again.

Another way of saying it. Perhaps words succeed us most in their failing.

*   *

NOTES

1. Peter Cole, *Poetry of Kabbalah: Mystical Verse from the Jewish Tradition* (New Haven: CT: Yale University Press, 2014), 7.

2. David Jasper, *The Secret Desert: Religion, Literature, Art, and Culture* (Blackwell Publishing, 2004), 19.

58 Bells

Within the contours of glass
                                    lives undone   questions alone
                    that live on: how to begin? And where?   Let's say
the desert. Let's say *the heart.* Let's say *heft of*   *bodies after*
                    they can't hold themselves up
                                    exhausted
        Let's say the words   the words fail to say

and sound
···

        A bell for memory,
                    a bell because
there is no memorial worthy, not really, only us, and the sun—

            When Thoreau's sister died, at her funeral, he opened a music box to
    the crowd
        then he walked
                                    outside. And so her music reaches on.
A bell for what humility can teach us. A bell because, I know, you tried—

            A bell transmuted through air
                        as we finally all are, stars.

A bell in the wind, saying your name and then another and another, then *sleep.*

A bell for the tower.
                        A bell for the reach.

        A bell rang out, over and over, under each

streetlight, neon, as speakers break out unknown notes in the chest—

                        A bell we lost count of, a bell we call *breach.*
A bell to remind my students to hold the door
                        a little longer, look each other
                                    in the eye—
A bell to signal the power of tiny gestures—
                            How much they might matter—

A bell named *siren,* the song   in the sound we can't stop

to weep. A bell for the words that just, no matter what, won't do—

A bell for the sobbing, stuck thuds we still make—a bell I wish I could forge then
    cast

          and ring for each and every single one

of you. A bell for our mistakes.   A bell to give it all up.   All that isn't decency.
    A bell to recuse

          by its virtue everything   that isn't gentleness
harmony startling us   back to our senses, humanity. A bell for *God*
                help me—

A bell like a token, a talisman, a totem—a bell that should never be used.

A bell because,   beauty. Because we woke up again, albeit in pain. A bell
    for all grace.
         A bell for the red rocks

                then the white rocks

                  a bell for the way

    the iron that gives them its name
        is the element we mourn here today.   A bell we don't need
to remind us the body is holy
        in body after body, so many
   bells the same.

A bell because, I don't know
        what to say—shattering truth remains, I couldn't move when I heard
    the news.
A bell sounded in my head every minute one year ago. A bell for the fracture.
    A bell for the bruise.
A bell for the ones we ignore—*please don't*—for every one loved and lost, a new bell
        we get to choose.

A bell for a colossus felled
        as a city onlooked.   A bell for the water, the depth that it took.

A bell, alone in a field—a bell that stays shook. Can we write down a life? How
    could we? And why? Who should—tonight the nuclear sun will set, but not
    everyone will look. So, the bell is a fugue.
         A sense of matter in the air—
    A bell is a figure, a bell in a book.

A bell for the resonance, the real music of *this*
            evening. For every minute we don't recognize
    that we move through   as one—

                                             a bell for the lucky who do

see the stuff we're made of. Strong. But not *too.*

                    A bell to remind us, in its vibrations, before this happened,
there was a month called *June.* How many bells
                                             must that be? Can you count them
Must'nt we, of needs? A bell for the improbability
                                        of country music.
Do you know there has never been a bell rung twice?
                    In the aftermath, the tone shifts, albeit unperceivably. Each
ring lets off some steam. Each sounding changes the scene.
                              A bell mutated of loss. A bell because there is no bell
          unchanged. A bell to move us, to alert every one.

A bell because—

all beauty, thought tattered, stays true. The way we won't look each other in the eye
      the same way
we used to. The way a boy held a door open, a half-minute longer, for all others
                                                    the next day.

A bell for the commons.

A bell for the ground.

A bell for the broken, and the pieces that we can't rend from the earth. Pieces we
      found. A bell
              for the earth.

A bell for no bell, because as Keats said, *to such music we've become a sod.* A bell for
      the band, our mothers, fathers, daughters, and sons. Let's call it a song. Let's say
      we stand
                                          together. For what

can we make of our loss and love but a resounding? And redemption and for so
      long, a paradise. What bell can we find to make up for even one voice, one
      second of one voice? A bell for no bells at all.

A bell for every prayer that won't ring out again. A bell for the bleeding, the holding,
      beginning—

A bell for this morning. I woke up and remembered something. A harmony, at
      remove. I opened my eyes and looked

at you.

Echo (Sangle)

So many world-departing

little resiliencies

make a home of the self

given half a chance

or opportunity—cleft

in the island off the horizon

holy interior chiasmus

not mine like the cry

or the perfect space between

your two perfect teeth

coming and going

        or as fog

fits exactly the sun

in its lap

sets

Echo (Heavy Water)

What so other
pulls so

rocks toward
shore

body down coast
line what winds

you know a lot
of things

before you
think

to say them

a lot of that stuff
stays core

maybe I didn't lose
as much as I thought

maybe more

what so other so
pulls rocks

and it is
here

this prayer
in answer

a day so pretty
I get worried again

about dying
what so other pulls

toward body
shore down coast
line what winds
home the self
so

Part Three

STRONGER TOGETHER

Vegas Golden Knights—Celebrating Heroes, Helping Las Vegas Heal

I remember coming in early Monday morning and everyone was already in the office, and it was eerily quiet. People were still in shock. We knew we had to do something. So, we talked among ourselves. What should we do with our players? How do we help without getting in the way?

–KERRY BUBOLZ, *president, Vegas Golden Knights*

We'd been together for three weeks as an organization with our players. What happened really impacted our players. Once we realized exactly what had happened, and the scope of things, there was a genuine interest our players had to want to help the city heal and deal with the tragedy.

–KELLY MCCRIMMON, *general manager (then assistant general manager), Vegas Golden Knights*

To see them out there and all they've been through the past week, it was a little nerve-wracking to speak in front of that many people. But the response from the crowd was phenomenal. It was the least we could do for those people that went through that. We want to get every win we can for the city and the people that were involved. When you get texts from the fire department saying the spirits are lifting around the department, it's crazy.

–DERYK ENGELLAND, *defenseman, Vegas Golden Knights*

You know he [Deryk Engelland] was very nervous, and he looked like he was calm, cool, and collected. And then he scored a goal.

–BILL FOLEY, *owner, Vegas Golden Knights*

12

1 October Memorial Committee

Five Years After—Reflections from Within

Tennille Pereira, Director of Vegas Strong Resiliency Center
and Chairwoman of the 1 October Memorial Committee

October 2, 2017. I woke to a cell phone brimming with text messages from across the country that were all basically the same: "Are you safe?" Confusion turned to horror as I logged into Facebook and then turned on the local news. The nation's largest modern mass shooting had taken place just miles from my home, and the images were awful and gut-wrenching. I stood frozen as it felt like the world I knew had just melted around me, and I knew in that moment that something had changed for me personally as well.

I knew I had to do something. I knew there was going to be a part for me to facilitate the healing within my community.

As Las Vegas began to wake up, news stations soon showed a number of images that would become as iconic for me as the empty cowboy boots left to litter the venue and sidewalks. There were lines of people wrapping around city blocks waiting to donate their blood to help, while others distributed handmade peanut butter and jelly sandwiches and water bottles to them. There were pallets of water and delivery after delivery of food brought to feed first responders and health-care workers working tirelessly to help the thousands of victims and survivors. In the days that followed, there would be fifty-eight handmade crosses rolling into town to be displayed under the iconic "Welcome to Fabulous Las Vegas" sign where thousands would visit and hold vigil to show solidarity and support. Two landscape architects would sit quietly in a café sketching a plan for a place of contemplation and solace, where thousands of community members would appear with an abundance of supplies and manpower to create a garden for healing. Las Vegas's expansion NHL team, the Vegas

Golden Knights, would dedicate their first regular-season home game to the first responders of 1 October and declare that "together, we are Vegas Strong."

Over the next few weeks, then months, then years, the term "Vegas Strong" would continue to ring throughout a community that was bound and determined to not let one horrific crime define it. October 1, 2017, was not just the day that the nation's largest recent mass shooting took place on the Las Vegas Strip, but the day that Las Vegas went from being a tourist destination to a solidified, strong community—a community left reeling and wounded, but determined to share its light. A community that now reached far beyond geographical borders.

Annually around October, I find myself reflecting on our community's journey, and my own journey, because they have intertwined from the beginning. I am awestruck again and again just as I was in those first days at the community's response and compassion. I am awestruck at the systemic changes within victim/survivor services that have expanded access and added abundant healing resources. I am awestruck at the individual healing stories among the survivors and bereaved families. I am awestruck at what the Vegas Strong Resiliency Center has been able to become.

My story with the Route 91 Harvest Festival shooting response began when I started staffing a legal assistance table in my role as an attorney with the Legal Aid Center of Southern Nevada at the Family Assistance Center ("Legal Aid"). I developed a plan with three daily shifts of volunteer attorneys and advocates from Legal Aid over the following several weeks. I took the first shift and soon realized that working with the families and the survivors of this tragedy was not going to be like anything I had ever experienced.

Once back at the office, I would reach out to anyone who had approached us and needed additional legal assistance. We were inundated with questions from the staff who worked the venue. They had not been paid what they were promised; and all of the tips, electronic and cash, had disappeared. Many legal issues involving many parties took months to unwind and resolve to get the workers justly paid.

A number of personal stories will forever stick with me and changed the kind of attorney I am and how I interact with those I serve. One of those clients was an elderly father of one of the victims, to whom I will refer as Robert. Robert had lost his adult daughter that night, and he was eager for an attorney's assistance in getting him the death certificate.

As an attorney, I have been trained to discover the issue at hand and devise a plan with the quickest route for redress for my client based on legal principles and my training. In my first meeting with Robert, I quickly realized this was *not* what he needed. What he truly needed was for me to set my pen down, settle into my seat, and *listen* to what he was telling me in so many ways. When I looked up, I saw a grieving father sitting across my desk asking for a death certificate that would declare his daughter had passed away on October 1, 2017, instead of October 2, 2017. If it stated that she passed on October 2, then Robert would have to envision his daughter dying over the course of a full day while she lay alone. This thought was too much for him to bear. No training had prepared me for this meeting and request. Knowing I likely could not draw on any legal authority or even pose a logical argument, I vowed to take up Robert's cause and do whatever I could.

Over the next several weeks, Robert requested several meetings with me. I would never turn him away. We would sit together in my office as he retold me his story. He was elderly and would ramble a bit about his daughter, his wife, and his daughter's only son, now left to navigate this world without his mom. He would describe his need to be there for them and what the loss meant to each of them. During those meetings, I learned to ignore my loudly clicking clock on the wall. I learned to ignore my colleagues as they watched through my window to see if I was available. I learned to turn my face away from the ever-growing inbox of emails. I did not point out any of the facts or logical points that would matter in his request. I learned to just listen as my degrees hung quietly on the wall, seemingly offering Robert some reassurance. I learned what it meant to share my humanity, and I am forever grateful to Robert and the many others who trusted me enough in those early days for this lesson.

I soon found myself with the executive director of Legal Aid, Barbara Buckley, in a meeting with federal consultants to discuss setting up what they called a "resiliency center." As consultants, they would facilitate the grant application process for an Antiterrorism and Emergency Assistance Program grant that is only available to communities responding to a mass violence incident. This particular grant is awarded based on the magnitude of the incident, the needs of the victims, and the local resources available at the time. The purpose of the grant is to bolster the community's existing resources and partnerships to meet the needs; however, it can also be used to develop or increase resources.

We walked out of that meeting in complete silence. Our minds raced at the possibilities that such a place could offer the affected community now, but also in perpetuity for any subsequent mass casualty incidents or other victims of violence. We knew that there were big holes in victim services at the time based on our work with victims before the shooting. We knew that many victims struggled to navigate a complicated, disjointed system and, quite often, were unable to access the services they needed for healing. This was *our* opportunity to make sure something good came out of this horrific crime.

We began by staffing a legal team at the newly formed Vegas Strong Resiliency Center (VSRC) that took over providing assistance from the Family Assistance Center. Soon, Clark County asked the Legal Aid Center of Southern Nevada, a more nimble nonprofit, to take over operations and management of the VSRC. We eventually moved into a newly renovated space to respond to survivors' needs with ample space for our community partners and collaborators to work alongside us and develop a community resource for healing. We began looking into victim services for the state of Nevada and whether changes could be made to facilitate healing for all victims. Two legislative sessions have come and gone and, during each one, we were able to consult and advise on successfully adopted measures that improved victim/survivor services throughout Nevada. In early 2021, the Office for Victims of Crime gave the prestigious National Crime Victims' Service Award to the Vegas Strong Resiliency Center, the first Nevada agency to be so honored. During the COVID-19 pandemic, we became a beacon in the storm for thousands now dealing with an extra layer of trauma. Just this past year, we were awarded an extra grant to hire a victim advocate to begin providing services to any victim of a violent crime in Nevada.

We would have never reached these important benchmarks without the like-minded efforts of national partners, local partners, and individuals throughout the survivor and bereaved family community. We would often find ourselves identifying a need and then looking for an appropriate resource to address it that simply did not exist, so we would turn to these trusted partnerships.

In the first days following the shooting, large donations helped survivors and bereaved families. About $22 million was either raised or committed and set aside until an appointed committee could decide how to divide it between bereaved families, physically injured survivors, and thousands of others left with unseen wounds. It was quickly apparent that there was never going to be enough money from that effort to meet the ever-growing needs of the tens of thousands affected in various ways. Eventually, that committee decided that all the bereaved families would receive a portion, and the remaining amount would be divided among the physically injured survivors. Anyone who believed they were a part of an impacted category could file a claim, but there was also a short time frame to do so. Unfortunately, all those reeling with unseen injuries would not receive any of the donated funds, and others who were unaware of the fund but qualified for it did not get the assistance either.

Day after day, we would take calls from survivors struggling to make ends meet after the trauma turned their lives upside down. Bartenders and waiters would describe their experiences working at the event and how their crippling fear prevented them from working. Families went through their savings and were not sure how to keep the lights on. Others were struggling to keep up with daily management of their lives, including their finances. Overwhelmingly apparent at the heart of the turmoil in each of their lives was an underlying need for some type of mental health resource. We had developed great collaborative partnerships throughout the community for mental health resources, but it was impossible to agree to connect when their financial issues were urgent and immediate. We began brainstorming ways to meet these needs and developed our emergency financial assistance program that gave us the ability to provide small amounts to meet emergent needs while we focused on providing longer-term healing resources.

To this day, all different types of professionals and businesses offer valuable resources or the development of resources to support the efforts of the vsrc. Behavioral health providers have increased their trauma resources. Survivors are trained to offer peer support to other survivors. Bereaved family members support one another through special social media connections they have established. Everywhere I turn, I see others rising to create, innovate, exceed, and strive to foster healing in themselves and in others.

In 2019, I was surprised to receive a phone call from Nevada governor Steve Sisolak asking if I would be willing to accept an appointment to the 1 October Memorial Committee that would be tasked with recommending a permanent memorial. I was extremely humbled by the request and grateful that I would be in a position to share all of the lessons we had learned about working with the Route 91 Harvest Festival family with those taking on this task.

The Las Vegas Community Healing Garden had been created through the efforts of many community partners in collaboration with bereaved families, survivors, and numerous community members. It had become a place of healing and comfort for tens of thousands. However, it was not planned or built as a permanent memorial designed to withstand the tests of time. It was also completed almost immediately after the incident and had not captured the community's complete healing journey.

The overall objective of the committee has always been to lead a healing process of community engagement. At the end of the process, we should have a recommendation for a proposal to place before the Clark County Commission. It has been a humbling process for me. I am not a public art professional, architect, or artist. I am an attorney at heart and often have strong opinions, but I was going to have to put my own desires to the side. The meetings are all open meetings. They are broadcast live through social media and a local television channel. The VSRC and its partners in California share the live stream through their extensive networks. Anyone can appear in person or online to make a comment or use the various social media feeds to share their thoughts. The meetings are often very emotional. The other committee members consist of a family member, an injured survivor, a first responder, an artist, an architect, and a public arts administrator—all with very different perspectives.

I would have to be real and vulnerable at times in a role that took me far out of my comfort zone on the public stage. To prepare us, Clark County Parks and Recreation facilitated several workshops that started after everything shut down because of the COVID-19 pandemic. It was surreal trying to come together as a committee and focus on such an important task while watching chaos ensue throughout the nation. We learned about the various groups affected by the tragedy, what assets were at our disposal, and the rules of open meetings. Most importantly, we made commitments to one another to show up and always honor the experiences of others.

At the first meeting, my peers voted for me to be the chairperson of the 1 October Memorial Committee. I was humbled, honored, and terrified all at the same time. Even after leading every subsequent monthly meeting since, I still feel humbled, honored, and terrified every time I take my seat to call the meeting to order. Before each meeting, I sit quietly in my car for just a moment to mentally prepare to be a conduit and facilitator. I learn something new every meeting about myself and others. The process develops more and more as we go along; it often feels like building an airplane while flying it. It can be easy to panic every once in a while, but I bring myself back and remember all the stories of light throughout the community, and I am reassured that it is going to work out. In the end, I know we will have something beautiful and healing for generations to remember not just what was lost, but what was gained—not just the evil, but the light.

It has also been an honor to take part in a bimonthly forum designed for Vegas Strong Resiliency Center directors by the National Mass Violence Victimization Research Center. These efforts have led to additional healing in all communities that have been devastated by mass violence. We have shared our experiences and learned from other communities from coast to coast to foster our collective healing.

Healing is not linear, and it does not happen in a vacuum. Setbacks are bound to happen along the way, and many of them come from circumstances outside of one's control. The same rings true for communities. Even absorbing the setbacks and various trials, looking back at this point, I am comforted to report that I truly see *healing*.

In a way, a community is coming together now as it did five years ago. The accumulation of all of the efforts, big and small, has led us down a path of healing five years in the making. I can honestly say that I am a better person, the community around me is more unified, victim/survivor services have improved, and healing has certainly taken place.

There is no finish line in this challenging and painful journey, yet I am confident that we will *continue to heal*, as we continue to foster healing in others.

13

The Las Vegas Community Healing Garden

Placemaking and the Death of "Sin City"

STEFANI EVANS, Oral Historian and Project Manager,
Oral History Research Center, UNLV Libraries

"Sin City" is a mythic place evoked by outsiders as shorthand for Las Vegas.[1] Sin City is also marketed from within by Southern Nevada's hospitality industry to entice nonresidents to visit and perhaps indulge in pleasures and sometimes vices illegitimate or ill-advised at home. Yet, to most Southern Nevadans, "Las Vegas" is not "Sin City"; it is simply the metropolitan place where they live and work. This chapter reflects on the public and private faces of metropolitan Las Vegas by examining everyday signs in the built environment. In particular, it focuses on the changing public perception of Las Vegas by considering the sign of the Las Vegas Community Healing Garden in the five days following October 1, 2017, the date of the largest mass shooting by an individual in modern American history.[2]

According to the theory of signs as structures of understanding, as put forth in 1964 by French literary theorist Roland Barthes, "Where there is a visual substance . . . the meaning is confirmed in a linguistic message."[3] Signs are physical; they refer to something else, and they are mutually used and recognized as signs. For example, the partnership between MGM Resorts International and concert producer Live Nation Entertainment that produced the annual Route 91 Harvest Festival events from 2014 to 2017 on the Las Vegas Strip also developed the festival's logo; the logo was, in turn, recognized by consumers as the "sign" of the concert. The round logo suggests an orange-and-white gaming chip on which is the US Route shield, the widely recognized marker used for US numbered highways, with a black "91" on the shield. While the numeral 91 on the US Route shield conveys a straightforward message to motorists, the accompanying visual image of the festival logo complicates and enhances its meaning. Thus, the linguistic and visual messages of US Highway 91 and the gaming chip work together to convey a message subsequently interpreted by the receiver as the "sign" of the Route 91 Harvest Festival in Las Vegas.

After the 1 October shooting, the Las Vegas Community Healing Garden became a sign of the humanity of Las Vegas. The garden's planning, construction, and its meaning are best viewed through the lens of placemaking. To architects, placemaking promotes "the complexity and seeming disorder of multifaceted neighborhoods, the layers of history and culture that make our cities the rich, interesting places they are."[4] In Las Vegas, placemaking came alive in the creation of the Las Vegas Community Healing Garden. Two landscape architects conceived the garden at a morning breakfast the day after the massacre, and City of Las Vegas officials determined its location. But from earthmoving to dedication—with all of the building materials, equipment, labor, living plants, and soils donated—it exemplified a bottom-up process of placemaking.

In a city known for automobile dependence, glittering signs, and hospitality and gaming industries, opportunities for placemaking are rare. In 1968, Yale University architects Robert Venturi, Denise Scott Brown, and Steven Izenour conducted a study to "learn from Las Vegas" the "iconography of urban sprawl." In their 1972 book, *Learning from Las Vegas,* the architects focused on a three-mile section of Las Vegas Boulevard, then designated US Route 91 and also known as the Las Vegas Strip. *Learning from Las Vegas* offered the first architectural acknowledgement of billboards (or signs) as "commercial architecture at the scale of the highway."[5] The architects noted that, rather than improving their properties, many Las Vegas Strip hotel owners instead periodically built bigger, brighter signs along the Strip to entice a larger share of automobile tourists from the highway and into their parking lots.[6]

In Southern Nevada, as in most places, jurisdiction matters. The City of Las Vegas, founded in 1905, predates Clark County's formation by four years. Clark County includes other incorporated municipalities as well as unincorporated towns. The 1 October shooting did not occur in Las Vegas boundaries; instead, it happened on private property in the unincorporated town of Paradise. The victims celebrated their music at Las Vegas Village, a barricaded fifteen-acre outdoor venue owned by MGM Resorts International. The shooter aimed his gun from the thirty-second floor of Mandalay Bay, also owned by MGM Resorts. Las Vegas Village is located diagonally across the Las Vegas Strip (the former US Route 91) from Mandalay Bay. The Las Vegas Strip, the Las Vegas Village, and Mandalay Bay all fall under the jurisdiction of Clark County, with the Clark County Commission its governing body.

Despite jurisdiction, successful memorials require public access because the public cannot spontaneously gather to mourn, heal, contemplate, or celebrate on private property, in a casino, or on a public highway. For these reasons, neither the concert venue, Mandalay Bay, nor the namesake US highway became the sign of the community response to the killings. The politics of commemoration and the nature of place-making explain why and how the Las Vegas Community Healing Garden became the public sign of 1 October and community healing and why it came to be in downtown Las Vegas.

Building the Garden

Toward the end of September 2017, forty-five years after *Learning from Las Vegas* legitimized Las Vegas billboards, twenty-two thousand country music fans from around the world congregated in Sin City. They arrived to enjoy the three-day Route 91 Harvest Festival. They packed cowboy boots, cowboy hats, sunglasses, and bandanas; sundresses, shorts, and jeans; and T-shirts and tank tops. They bought transportation, lodging, meals, and concert tickets, and they enthusiastically supported the merchants who ringed the venue. They danced and they sang, and they enjoyed themselves, the music, Las Vegas, and each other. They also planned to return home.

On Sunday, October 1, the festival's third and final night, ticket holders gathered to hear their favorite songs and their favorite musicians. As cheering fans greeted singer Jason Aldean as he stepped on the stage just after 10:05 p.m., a solitary figure across the street and thirty-two floors above quietly aimed his weapon at the dancing crowd, deliberately tightened his finger on the trigger, and, during the next ten minutes, sprayed more than one thousand bullets into the people below. The security fencing surrounding the venue barricaded the targets inside and impeded their flight. Fifty-eight people died within hours; two more suffered from their injuries for up to three years before dying of them.[7] Almost nine hundred people sustained physical injuries, including more than four hundred hit by gunshot or shrapnel.[8] Thousands more were psychologically wounded by the shooting and its aftermath. Over time, more Route 91 Harvest Festival survivors will succumb to the damage that the shooting and its aftermath inflicted on their bodies.

As the city and the nation awoke the next morning to news of the tragedy, local landscape architects Jay Pleggenkuhle and Daniel Perez met for breakfast and decided to create a publicly accessible place where their traumatized city could freely gather and begin to heal. Because they had a working relationship with Las Vegas city attorney Brad Jerbic, they called Jerbic to ask for city-owned space where they could create a temporary pop-up garden. The architects then had no idea that the attorney and his office colleagues were reeling from reports that their beloved young colleague, Cameron Robinson, whom coworkers often teased for his love of country music, had been shot and killed at the concert. Jerbic invited Pleggenkuhle and Perez to his office.

Thus, it happened that on Monday afternoon, less than seventeen hours after the bullets stopped, a grieving City of Las Vegas bureaucracy granted land to build a permanent healing garden in response to a mass murder that occurred in another jurisdiction. Perez sketched the design on the back of his restaurant menu. He visualized a grove of trees, one tree for each departed soul, surrounding a mature oak tree—the Tree of Life—as though to embrace and protect it. True to the design, the Tree of Life shelters the garden and thrives in a heart-shaped planter at the garden's center. The planter represents the heart of the garden and the community; its top of broken red tiles provides seating and conveys our collective broken heart.[9] Like most human creations, the garden is imperfect. While the number of trees was intended to be symbolic, each of the original fifty-eight bereaved families spontaneously "adopted" a specific tree to honor their deceased loved one, leaving the two subsequent deaths unrepresented.

Pleggenkuhle's description of the garden's conception and its creation employs terms that reflect the organic, bottom-up concept of placemaking. He recalls, "With sunrise on Tuesday, a miracle began. Materials and donations started to appear. Together, hundreds of people planted trees and flowers. They built pathways and a remembrance wall. They hugged and cried. They shared their stories and bared their souls. By

Friday evening, the miracle had occurred. A crude yet beautiful garden was complete. But even more miraculous than the garden was the presence of love and hope that flowed through it."[10] On Friday evening, October 6, city and state officials dedicated the Las Vegas Community Healing Garden.

In normal times, the meanings of signs evolve over time, regionally, and across race and class. However, in the ten minutes after 10:05 p.m., Sunday, October 1, 2017, shock and trauma radically altered the iconic signs of Las Vegas. Within hours, social media had transformed "Sin City" Las Vegas into "#VegasStrong," a new hashtag suggesting sympathy and support.[11] Local tattoo parlors offered Vegas-themed tattoos to benefit victims' funds.[12] Las Vegas Strip casinos quickly modified their electronic signage in support of victims and first responders.[13] By the Friday evening dedication of the healing garden, even the mayor's podium featured the new #VegasStrong hashtag just below the city seal.[14]

Likewise, bereaved family, survivors, friends, and allies quickly began modifying and repurposing the Route 91 Harvest Festival logo by adding a wing to each side to signify the incomprehensible loss of human life, the death of the festival, and the mourning and healing of families and survivors. Almost four years after the killings, on August 2, 2021, the Clark County Commission announced that MGM Resorts International planned to donate two acres of the fifteen-acre concert venue for a permanent memorial to honor the victims of 1 October.[15] Until Clark County dedicates its memorial, the Las Vegas Community Healing Garden, created through placemaking within the boundaries of the City of Las Vegas, remains the sole site of 1 October commemoration. Even with the welcome addition of the Clark County memorial, the garden will continue to be the sign of the Las Vegas community's response to the tragedy, a bottom-up, permanent, and tranquil place for hope, healing, and remembrance.

The Garden's Being

From the moment that donations and volunteers arrived at the site, and in the four years since its dedication, the Las Vegas Community Healing Garden has become the tangible sign to the world of a resilient and loving Las Vegas. The garden is distinctly urban, a one-quarter acre in downtown Las Vegas, bounded by a major street, an alley, a driveway, and a parking lot. A bus stop marks the front. The garden is also distinctly Las

Vegas: it sits just north of an adult entertainment boutique. Get Outdoors Nevada, a nonprofit organization, maintains the Las Vegas Community Healing Garden to serve "as a place of calm to remember those touched by tragedy" and to provide "a place of refuge for healing." The interactive garden has become the sign for our evolving memories of 1 October. It is not simply a garden in isolation. It is the sign that celebrates the "life, compassion, and fellowship that we find in community."[16]

Get Outdoors Nevada hosts annual memorial services and regularly scheduled planting, rock-painting, and cleanup events. It also curates mementos and messages left by visitors, periodically rotating them to ensure that the garden remains well kept and welcoming over time. These events harness the hearts and creativity of diverse stakeholders—Clark County church and school groups; social, business, and fraternal organizations; neighboring residents and businesses; and survivors and bereaved families. Together, they accomplish the shared goals of celebrating the departed, comforting the bereaved, honoring the survivors, and promoting community healing through communal ownership.

Near the top of the heart-shaped planter that houses the Tree of Life, five panels of increasing size form an interactive wall that frames the garden and invites visitors to leave mementos and messages. These permanent installations replaced the temporary wall that stood for the dedication. Clockwise from left, the first panel features framed faces of the souls who departed in the hours after the murder. The next offers a brief narrative of the shooting and the community response, explaining, "This time, we as a community pushed back with a very deliberate act of compassion." The central panel, Remembrance Wall, displays raised, polished, brass bars, suitable for rubbings, each bearing the name of a life taken by the shooter. Next, a wall of falling water symbolizes life and renewal and emits a soothing, hypnotic, bubbling effect that accompanies the rhythms of the city. The largest panel offers a verse from Shakespeare's *Romeo and Juliet* set amid star-shaped cutouts: "When he shall die / Take him and cut him out in little stars / And he will make the face of heaven so fine / That all the world will be in love with night / And pay no worship to the garish sun."[17]

Like the best and most effective memorials, the urban garden built through placemaking embraces all who have experienced trauma or loss by allowing them to experience nature and begin to heal.

The Garden's Meaning

The volunteers who built the garden and the visitors who seek its comfort knew what they wanted the garden to be and what they wanted to find in it. Yet, as it took shape, the garden became something no one could have predicted: it became the sign of a city with a soul. Lifetime resident and second-generation architect Joy Rineer tried to describe the Las Vegas she'd always known, the one stripped of its Sin City costume and suddenly naked to the world: "We are a strong community. We are a small-knit community. We're a community with incredibly deep roots and identity. . . . We're big and we're little all at the same time. People see only the big. They see only the billboards. . . . Yes, we're *that*. But we're so much more; we're *this*."[18]

While most cities highlight a public face to attract tourists and business, Las Vegas does it better than most. Absent from Las Vegas marketing campaigns, though, are the local residents that reflect a tightly knit, diverse, vibrant, and generous Las Vegas community—the *this* that Rineer values even as she acknowledges our *that*. In contrast, *that* is trope of the Sin City promoted by the Las Vegas Convention and Visitors Authority and vaulted into popular culture over and over in books, on television, and in films. Books that captured the public's imagination included *The Green Felt Jungle* (1962), *Fear and Loathing in Las Vegas* (1971), *Learning from Las Vegas (1972),* and *Leaving Las Vegas* (1990). Television shows like *Vega$* (1978–81), *CSI: Crime Scene Investigation* (2000–2015), *Pawn Stars* (2009–present), and *Queen of Hearts* (2014–present), brought Sin City into living rooms. However, beginning with *Las Vegas Nights* (1941) and *The Las Vegas Story* (1952), movies of every genre projected indelible images of Las Vegas as Sin City to audiences of all ages including *Meet Me in Las Vegas* (1956), *Ocean's Eleven* (1960, the remake in 2001, and *Ocean's Thirteen,* 2007), *Viva Las Vegas* (1964), *Diamonds Are Forever* (1971), *The Gauntlet* (1977), *Rain Man* (1988), *Bugsy* (1991), *Honeymoon in Vegas* (1992), *Indecent Proposal* (1993), *Leaving Las Vegas* (1995), *Casino* (1995), *Con Air* (1997), *Vegas Vacation* (1997), *Fear and Loathing in Las Vegas* (1998), *The Cooler* (2003), *The Hangover* (2009), *Last Vegas* (2013), and *Jason Bourne* (2016).

The community response to 1 October cloaked signs of Sin City to reveal Rineer's *this:* the close community that gathered together in brokenness to offer blood, counseling, faith, fellowship, food, furnishings, love, money, prayers, scholarships, shelter, and unity. It is *this,* the humane and human Las Vegas, that harnessed its grief through the process of placemaking and in just five days built a place to mourn, remember, and heal. The Las Vegas Community Healing Garden is the sign and the physical embodiment of what Southern Nevadans have always known and what the world learned after 1 October 2017: we are Las Vegas, and Las Vegas is us.

NOTES

1. This chapter uses "Las Vegas" for the Las Vegas metropolitan area and "City of Las Vegas" and "the City" to refer to the incorporated city. For "den of sin," see, for example, Pacific Ancient and Modern Language Association, 2020 (2021) Conference Theme, "City of God, City of Destruction," https://www.pamla.org/conference-theme-city-of-god-city-of-destruction/.

2. For jurisdictional division between the City of Las Vegas and the County of Clark, see "Birth of a Railroad Town, 1902–1910," Chapter 2, in Eugene Moehring and Michael S. Green, *Las Vegas: A Centennial History,* Wilbur S. Shepperson Series in Nevada History (Reno and Las Vegas: University of Nevada Press, 2005), 23–36.

3. Roland Barthes, translated by Annette Lavers and Colin Smith, "Introduction," in *Elements of Semiology* (1964; 1st American edition, New York: Hill and Wang, 1968), unpaginated.

4. Debra Webb, "Placemaking and Social Equity: Expanding the Framework of Creative Placemaking," *Artivate* 3, no. 1 (Winter 2014): 16.

5. Robert Venturi, Denise Scott Brown, and Steven Izenour, *Learning from Las Vegas* (1972; rev. ed., Cambridge, MA: MIT Press, 1977), 6.

6. Venturi, Brown, and Izenour, xii, 51–53.

7. Darcy Spears, "How did 1 October shooting deaths increase officially to 60 victims?" *13 Investigates,* KTNV Las Vegas, 1 October 2020; https://www.ktnv.com/13-investigates/how-did-1-october-shooting-deaths-increase-officially-to-60-victims.

8. Joseph Lombardo, sheriff, *LVMPD Criminal Investigative Report of the 1 October Mass Casualty Shooting: LVMPD Event Number 171001–3519* (Las Vegas: Las Vegas Metropolitan Police Department, August 3, 2018), 19; pdf, https://www.lvmpd.com/en-us/Documents/1-October-FIT-Criminal-Investigative-Report-FINAL_080318.pdf.

9. Jay Pleggenkuhle, as quoted in Stefani Evans and Donna McAleer, eds., *Healing Las Vegas: The Las Vegas Community Healing Garden in Response to the 1 October Tragedy* (Reno: University of Nevada Press, 2019), 12, 13. Regarding the trope of sketching on a napkin, Perez actually drew his design on the back of a menu, but when a story came out that he had drawn it on a napkin, the architects opted not to correct it publicly for the sake of consistency.

10. Pleggenkuhle, quoted in *Healing Las Vegas,* 12, 13.

11. "Selected Tweets," *Healing Las Vegas,* 85. Three of the four tweets include a version of the hashtag #VegasStrong.

12. "3 Places to Get a Las Vegas Tattoo That Benefits Victim Fund," *Las Vegas Review-Journal,* October 7, 2017, accessed November 20, 2021; https://www.reviewjournal.com/local/local-las-vegas/3-places-to-get-a-las-vegas-tattoo-that-benefits-victim-fund/.

13. "Las Vegas Strip Shares Unifying 'Vegas Strong' Message," KTNV Las Vegas, October 3, 2017; https://www.ktnv.com/news/las-vegas-strip-shares-unifying-vegas-strong-message.

14. Jennifer Burkhart and Ryan Reason, SquareShooting.com, "Mayor Goodman Dedicating Las Vegas Community Healing Garden," October 6, 2017; City of Las Vegas, *Flickr* item 20171006-healinggardenopen-15_36946395364_0_29010807208_0.

15. Rio Lacanlale, "MGM Donates Land for Route 91 Memorial to Be Built at Site of Shooting," *Las Vegas Review-Journal,* August 2, 2021, https://www.reviewjournal.com/local/local-las-vegas/mgm-donates-land-for-route-91-memorial-to-be-built-at-site-of-shooting-2411954/.

16. "Las Vegas Community Healing Garden," *Get Outdoors Nevada,* https://getoutdoorsnevada.org/lv-healing-garden/.

17. From William Shakespeare, *Romeo and Juliet,* Act III, Scene II.

18. Joy Rineer, quoted in *Healing Las Vegas,* 65.

14

Preserving Community Grief

The Remembering 1 October Collection at the Clark County Museum

Cynthia Sanford, Registrar, Clark County Museum

One of the most important roles of a museum in a community is to preserve and present the history and culture of that community. This usually comes in the form of soliciting donations of historical items and constructing exhibits around those items. Increasingly, however, museums are expected to collect and curate contemporary ephemera representing current events. This "rapid response" collecting often comes about because of tragic events that affect the community. The Clark County Museum in Henderson was faced with such a project when tasked with collecting and preserving the tribute items left at a spontaneous memorial in honor of the victims of the mass shooting on the Las Vegas Strip on October 1, 2017.

Almost immediately after the shooting, makeshift memorials appeared throughout the area, some with the support of local government. The memorials took many forms: small groups of candles and flowers; professionally printed banners and signs; graffiti on walls. Each of these memorials meant something to the people who created or added to them. One of the largest memorials was erected at the iconic "Welcome to Fabulous Las Vegas" sign on the Las Vegas Strip, not far from the massacre. This memorial was created around white painted crosses dedicated to the victims, created by a man who had commemorated tragedies like these all over the country. Once the crosses were installed, thousands of people—locals and visitors—began to leave tribute items at the site.

Located at one of the most visited spots in the tourist corridor, this memorial created a difficult dilemma for county officials—how to balance public safety concerns against the obvious need of the community to grieve after such a tragedy, at a time when there were far more important issues to address. Officials faced many questions: How long should the memorial stay in place? What should happen to the tens of thousands of items that people left? Who should be responsible for making decisions about the memorial? Who are the stakeholders, and what rights should they have? How does a city whose entire identity is built around having fun deal with this visual representation of tragedy positioned at one of its most iconic spots?

Eventually, officials determined a time limit for the memorial and assigned county workers the job of maintaining both the memorial and public safety. They also decided that transferring the tribute items to a museum was the ideal solution after the memorial was removed. After all, museums are responsible for preserving the history of the community, and that history includes grief and mourning.

Public displays of grief have always been part of human history. One need only to look at some of the most famous structures in history to see examples. The pyramids built in ancient Egypt were not only final resting places for pharaohs, but unavoidable reminders of their lives and deaths. The Taj Mahal in India, built as a mausoleum in the seventeenth century, is visited by millions of people today. Museums are also full of smaller representations of grief, from Victorian mourning jewelry to Day of the Dead costumes. Over the years, cultures created unique death rituals and ways of sharing grief within the community. These resulted in artifacts that museums use to tell the history of death and mourning through the centuries.

Many people trace the beginnings of modern spontaneous public memorials, at least in the United States, to the opening of the Vietnam Veterans Memorial in Washington, DC, in 1982. The Vietnam War was the first "televised" war, which frequently exposed the public to images of violent death. This, along with mixed and passionate public opinion on the war, meant that the community was grieving, looking for a way to express that grief. Here was a memorial that shared similarities with cemeteries, a familiar place to grieve, but also impressed upon the visitor the scale of loss. It became a place for people to publicly express the grief that may have previously been kept private. This led people to leave items with private meanings, specific to one of the names on the memorial wall, and items that were meant as a public expression of grief and remembrance, as much for those who visited the wall after them as for the dead memorialized there. It provided not just an outlet for grief, but possibly a representation of community, a shared grief with friends and strangers alike. The memorial is part of the US National Park Service, which preserves some of the items left there to tell the history of the memorial and the people who grieved there.

Another important event in the modern history of public mourning was the death of Princess Diana in 1997. Here again was violent, unexpected death, which was covered extensively by the news media. In most people's memory, this was the first time that large-scale memorials with offerings similar to those left at the Vietnam Veterans Memorial were created spontaneously in public spaces related to the incident. Most of these tribute items were flowers, which could not be saved by museums. Anything that could be saved was donated to hospitals or charitable organizations. After the Columbine High School shooting in Colorado in 1999, the memorial for the victims was a common visual in the background of news reports about the massacre. This shooting not only shaped how future events were covered by the media, but also cemented the importance of impromptu memorials in the public grieving process. While some of the items left at the memorial were saved, the community eventually decided to create a permanent memorial to victims of the shooting. The terrorist attacks on September 11, 2001, was such a momentous event that memorials spread to places that were not specifically related to what had happened, and spontaneous memorials appeared throughout the country and the world. A multimillion-dollar museum was created to memorialize the site, and its collection and exhibits include tribute items left at various places throughout the area. Smaller museums and libraries across the county also collected and preserved items left at local memorials.

As these memorials became more common, institutions began to recognize that the memorials were important, not just to the people who were directly affected by the tragedies, but also to the community as a whole. With more mass shootings, and therefore more memorials, we could see the similarities in how people reacted. While each memorial was specific to the event and city, they shared fundamental similarities. They were made up of thousands of flowers, candles, cards, and stuffed animals; items with personal meanings and items that represented mourning in general. Bits of ephemera that seem unimportant when taken at face value. But each item tells an individual story, and examined as a whole, the items demonstrate an important aspect of modern American culture.

On October 9, eight days after the shooting on the Las Vegas Strip, the first tribute items were delivered to the Clark County Museum for safekeeping. These were items that were deemed to be fragile or potentially dangerous and had to be removed from the memorial site. The museum offered to accept them so that they wouldn't have to be destroyed. Soon after, it was determined that the museum would be saving everything possible from the memorial at the "Welcome to Fabulous Las Vegas" sign, so that the items left by those mourning the tragedy could be preserved.

The memorial at the iconic sign remained in place for six weeks. The "Welcome" sign, on a median strip of Las Vegas Boulevard South, has limited space for a memorial. To keep the memorial from overflowing the median, encroaching on a heavily trafficked road, and to make room for more, county workers had to remove items from almost the first week of the memorial's existence. The museum received deliveries twice each week while the memorial was in place. It is impossible to estimate how many individual items were left at the memorial. The majority were flowers and floral arrangements, which the museum was unable to preserve. Staff and dedicated volunteers catalogued, photographed, and housed everything that could be saved from the memorial, which resulted in about 18,000 items added to the museum's collections. Additionally, the museum received 4,500 items sent to local hospitals, fire departments, and police departments. This project took 9,000 hours, and the resulting collection takes up more than 450 square feet of storage space.

The items left at the memorial were the same familiar items left at every memorial, cemetery, and roadside cross. There were flowers, stuffed animals, candles, and similar small objects. Some people left a single item, and others left one for each of the fifty-eight crosses representing the victims. Some of the items were mass-produced—things that people purchased at nearby stores or brought with them to their vacation in Las Vegas. Others were specifically made, commissioned by survivors of the shooting or others who felt particularly affected. These included posters and banners, a set of dog tags created as part of an event raising money for the victims, and special pamphlets from local churches and religious groups. Some businesses, both in the local area and from around the country, left items. Many people handcrafted small items to leave at the memorial. This allowed them to channel their grief through their skills and talents and add to the public outpouring of grief. Several paintings were done as part of organized classes that combined painting and drinking wine, which demonstrated how this shooting permeated so many aspects of life in the Las Vegas area. Others left cards and letters, both sharing their grief and offering comfort to others. Many schools sent cards made by children, some of which were sympathetic in general, and others which were very specific about the shooting and its aftermath. Many of the items represented county music and related themes, since the shooting occurred at a country music festival. There were also items representing Las Vegas left at the memorial. Many people left ticket stubs from concerts and events, souvenir items from Las Vegas, and even hotel room key cards. One man left a token he had won at a poker tournament in town. Finally, there were items left by survivors of the shooting and friends and families of the victims. These were often very personal and had specific and sometimes unknown meanings to those who left them. The one thing that all of these items had in common, regardless of the type of item they were or the meaning behind them, was that they represented how people were mourning this tragedy, both as individuals and as a community.

The purpose of this collection, indeed the purpose of every museum collection, is to tell a story. The museum needed to be able to tell the story of the memorial and what it meant to the community. Therefore, in addition to collecting tribute items, the museum also collected stories. We asked anyone who had left items at the memorial to tell us what they left and why they felt it was important to do so. This allowed the museum to not only show how the community reacted to a tragedy, but also why they reacted in that way, and also justified the museum's involvement.

Many questioned the tribute items' inclusion in the Clark County Museum's collections. It was important for the museum to understand the importance of the memorial to the community and to justify it as representational of the community's history. Obviously, the memorial was important to those most affected by the tragedy—the friends and families of the victims. According to a study conducted by University of Dayton sociology professor Art Jipson, in which he interviewed 309 people involved with erecting memorials after the death of a loved one, every person interviewed felt that the memorial was more meaningful to them than the gravestone in the cemetery.[1] This was on display in Las

Vegas as well. Many friends and family members of victims spoke with me or visited the museum to see items left at the memorial. They were all grateful that the museum was preserving these items. They saw this as a way for their loved ones to be remembered and were comforted by knowing that the items left at the memorial would be preserved and shared.

The memorial items were also important to people who were not directly affected by the shooting. People who left items at the memorial for the victims, volunteers who were processing the collections, and museum visitors offered a common sentiment: they just wanted to "do something." Many people were looking for a productive outlet for their grief, and that took the form of creating tribute items and leaving them at a public memorial. This was often done in addition to donating money to appropriate fundraising efforts, providing assistance to those in need, and donating blood in the immediate aftermath of the shooting. While on the surface these reactions seem more useful, they didn't have the same emotional effect as leaving an offering at a memorial. Grieving in such a public way gave individuals an outlet for their grief and made them feel like part of a community, dealing with a tragedy together.

The tribute items left at the memorial, and the memorial itself, were therefore very important to individuals. The memorial also became a visual representation of a community coming together and offered proof that this community exists, even in a city like Las Vegas that is so often represented as simply a hedonistic escape for the rest of the world. Even for those who did not leave anything at the memorial, it was a reminder that there was a community, and that we were all grieving together. This feeling of community was an important aspect of the reaction to the shooting, and documenting it was an essential way to preserve this story for the future.

Finally, the memorial, and all similar memorials demonstrate how we, as individuals in the twenty-first century, grieved. This is why it is so important for museums and other cultural institutions to collect items from the memorials. Rather than an example of a specific event, it is part of a continuum of changing cultural expressions. It is part of the history of public expressions of grief. Candles and stuffed animals may not be as impressive as pyramids, but they are all part of the same story: the history of human grieving and human society in general. While it is often difficult to understand history as it is happening, it is clear that the memorials represent something important to us as a society, and future generations will thank us for acting to preserve artifacts to tell this story.

NOTES

1. Arthur Jipson, *Roadside Memorials in the Community: A Scientific Study of Roadside Memorials*, 2009. Retrieved from http://graphics8.nytimes.com/images/blogs /roomfordebate/Roadside_Memorial.pdf.

15

A Moment of Silence
Is No Longer Enough

Working to Address the Plague of Gun Violence

DINA TITUS, US Representative, Nevada's First Congressional District

When the phone rings in the middle of the night, you know it cannot be good news. Such was the case on October 1, 2017. As the representative for the district where the deadliest mass shooting in modern US history occurred, after rushing to Las Vegas Metro Police's command center and being briefed on the unfolding situation, I was unsure how to proceed. I wanted to be helpful, but not to get in the way. I wanted to express my sympathy, but not to intrude on the victims' and their families' privacy. And I wanted to tell the world what was going on and how outraged I was, but not to appear as though I were capitalizing on a tragedy for political purposes.

In the end, my team chose to work quietly behind the scenes to provide services that some might dismiss as menial or even overlook altogether but proved to make a real difference in the wake of the massacre. For example, we helped locate, identify, and return articles such as purses, cell phones, backpacks, and even shoes left behind in the panic. We helped the undocumented and frightened apply for and receive assistance. We intervened on behalf of international visitors who needed visa extensions. We worked with Clark County and the Internal Revenue Service to set up a victims' assistance fund. We distributed water and snacks to the thousands waiting in long lines to donate desperately needed blood. We delivered meals to hospital workers and first responders. And we fielded calls from around the world trying to find out the state of their loved ones who might have been in attendance that night.

We were not alone. Few visitors seldom venture beyond the Fabulous Strip or see beyond the bright lights, so they do not think of Las

Vegas as a place with a sense of community. Nothing could be further from the truth. In the days following the shooting, people came together in shared grief and grit like never imagined. They were inspired by the acts of heroism that night by those in attendance and those first on the scene: people shielding strangers with their own bodies and carrying the fallen to shelter under a rain of bullets; driving the wounded to hospitals in private vehicles and applying life-saving measures with belts and scarves. The emergency medical technicians, doctors, nurses, and medical staff operated in wartime, *M*A*S*H*-like conditions as hundreds of wounded poured in.

In the early morning when the unbelievable news broke, people were in shock and rushed to donate blood. Hotels offered complimentary rooms for those who had to stay in town with injured family members and those who came to town to sadly collect remains and make final arrangements. Restaurants provided meals for frontline workers. Churches, social organizations, labor unions, and local businesses all pitched in however they could be helpful. Ordinary people reached deep in their pockets to contribute to the victims' fund, and service centers were quickly established to provide counseling and other logistical assistance. A shrine was erected, and everyone kept asking, "Why?"

There is no answer. The shooter was killed at the scene. He died along with innocent revelers who had gone to a concert for an evening of fun. Found in his possession was a cache of AR-15 style guns, high-capacity magazines, bump stocks, and hundreds of rounds of ammunition he had secretly transported to his hotel room on the thirty-second floor of Mandalay Bay. No motive was ever established.

The public, pundits, and politicians all expressed outrage at yet another senseless act of gun violence. There was once again a moment of silence on the floor of the House of Representatives with thoughts and prayer offered up by the members. If the events at Sandy Hook, Emanual AME Church, and the Pulse nightclub were not enough, surely this mass tragedy would provoke real reform.

I immediately introduced an anti–bump stock bill to outlaw the easily obtainable attachments used by the shooter that allow a semi-automatic weapon to fire more rapidly. There was a lot of hue and cry about the bill, opposed by the powerful National Rifle Association, and no legislation was passed. The Bureau of Alcohol, Tobacco, and Firearms issued a rule equating bump stocks with machine guns, but, as projected, a court immediately struck it down. The decision was appealed, and the

US Court of Appeals for the Sixth Circuit in an 8–8 ruling allowed the regulation to stand. Backed by twenty-two state attorneys general, it is now being appealed to the US Supreme Court. Given the Supreme Court's June 23, 2022, ruling in *New York State Rifle & Pistol Association v. Bruen,* it seems likely the ATF rule will be struck down.

Meanwhile, the issue moved to the states. In the 2019 session, under the leadership of Assemblywoman Sandra Jauregui, who was at the October 1, 2017, festival, the Nevada Legislature passed expanded background checks for private party sales. It also passed AB291, which banned bump stocks and implemented an Extreme Risk or "red flag" law enabling family and law enforcement to act when a person poses a threat to themselves or others with a firearm. Similar legislation to reduce gun violence and keep guns out of the hands of dangerous individuals has been signed into law in a number of states. Nineteen states plus the District of Columbia have red flag laws, and eleven plus the District have bump stock bans. These laws, however, are now in jeopardy of being overturned.

Following two additional attention-grabbing mass shootings in spring 2022, one in a Buffalo grocery store killing ten people and another in a Texas grammar school where nineteen children and two teachers were mowed down, the House passed a package of gun safety measures on June 8. This package included my bump stock bill, which was supported by all Democrats and thirteen Republicans. The Senate rejected the package and put forth its own much watered-down bill, which did not include any bump stock restrictions. The House concurred and hopefully, this law will save lives and be the first step toward greater gun violence prevention reform.

As I have worked for enactment of legislation, I also secured federal funding for the Legal Aid Center of Southern Nevada to help our community heal, specifically to establish the Vegas Strong Resiliency Center. We continue to face challenges responding to the needs of those directly and indirectly affected by the events of 1 October, and this center will provide vital support for families and survivors as they process grief and strive to recover. It is our hope that the work we do in Las Vegas can serve as a model for other communities.

During the president's annual State of the Union address to Congress, I always leave my guest seat vacant, marked with a black ribbon, in memory of the 1 October victims. But that is not enough. Our community, along with the others scarred by gun violence, will continue fighting until we have made real progress in addressing this deadly plague.

16

Documenting and
Reflecting on 1 October

A Selected Bibliography of Collections and Scholarship

Priscilla Finley and Su Kim Chung, University Libraries, UNLV

Within days of the attack on attendees of the Route 91 Harvest Festival in 2017, officials from University Libraries at the University of Nevada, Las Vegas, met with Southern Nevada cultural heritage organizations to determine the best way to document the responses to the tragic events of 1 October and the #VegasStrong movement. The organizations included the Nevada State Museum, the Clark County Museum, the Las Vegas News Bureau (a division of the Las Vegas Convention and Visitors Authority), and the National Museum of Organized Crime and Law Enforcement (the Mob Museum).

The museums agreed to gather physical artifacts resulting from the aftermath, and UNLV Special Collections and Archives would be responsible for collecting documentary sources related to the event, including web content, Twitter posts, and oral histories. With the help of Archive-It, a service of the Internet Archive, firsthand testimonies from attendees and first responders, photographs and videos of the event and the subsequent outpouring of community support, and related news coverage have been preserved. Using a command line tool called twarc developed by the Documenting the Now project, Special Collections and Archives captured millions of tweets from and about the event.

The UNLV University Libraries' Oral History Research Center collected and preserved firsthand testimonies from first responders, witnesses, and survivors. Individuals were invited to submit their digital photographs, videos, or memories of the event and its aftermath, the victims and survivors, the community response, and the vigils and commemorations to the UNLV University Libraries collections.

Campus events were recorded and archived, and many UNLV faculty and researchers responded by adapting their research agendas to apply their disciplinary lens to the event. This selected bibliography surveys physical and digital collections, memorials, communications, and scholarship analyzing the event.

UNLV Special Collections and Archives

https://special.library.unlv.edu.

Alam, Miranda. "October 1 Vigil Photographs." Photo collection, 2017. PH-00405. Special Collections and Archives, University Libraries, University of Nevada, Las Vegas. https://special.library.unlv.edu/ark:/62930/f1fd21. Forty-seven digital photographs taken by Miranda Alam in 2017 of vigils held around Las Vegas after the October 1, 2017, mass shooting. The locations included the "Welcome to Fabulous Las Vegas" sign and the Las Vegas Community Healing Garden.

Olson, Tanya. *Forever in Our Hearts Documentary,* 2018. MS-00909. Special Collections and Archives, University Libraries, University of Nevada, Las Vegas. A short documentary film that highlights the Las Vegas Community Healing Garden, a memorial established after 1 October. The film is composed of photographs taken by Tanya Olson, a graduate of the University of Nevada, Las Vegas.

Remembering 1 October Oral History Project, 2017–2019. Special Collections and Archives, University Libraries, University of Nevada, Las Vegas. https://special.library .unlv.edu/ark%3A/62930/f1hr1q. After 1 October, the UNLV University Libraries' Oral History Research Center launched an oral history project to collect and preserve firsthand testimonies from first responders, witnesses, and survivors.

Steve Round Memorial Book of the 1 October Shooting in Las Vegas, 2017. MS-00853. Special Collections and Archives, University Libraries, University of Nevada, Las Vegas. https://special.library.unlv.edu/ark%3A/62930/f1pw4s. This collection is composed of a memorial book filled with handwritten condolences, memorials, and prayers for the victims of the mass shooting that occurred on October 1, 2017. From October 2 through October 10, Round watched over a memorial that spontaneously developed in the median of Las Vegas Boulevard South near the site of the shooting. Round invited visitors at the memorial, including families and friends of the victims, community members, first responders, and tourists, to sign the book.

University of Nevada, Las Vegas #VegasStrong Banner, 2017. UA-00077. Special Collections and Archives, University Libraries, University of Nevada, Las Vegas. https:// special.library.unlv.edu/ark:/62930/f1p145. The UNLV #VegasStrong Banner is a vinyl banner depicting a silhouette of the Las Vegas skyline. The banner includes signatures and messages written by students in memory of the 2017 mass shooting.

Web Archive on the October 1, 2017, Shooting in Las Vegas, Nevada. MS-00866. Special Collections and Archives, University Libraries, University of Nevada, Las Vegas. https://special.library.unlv.edu/. This project captured websites and Twitter data related to the shooting. Captured websites are primarily composed of articles and news stories from local, national, and international news media outlets. Websites were captured periodically from 2017 to 2018. The collection also includes Twitter data associated with the shooting that were captured via concurrent queries to the Twitter API for all Tweets containing the term "vegas" occurring September 29, 2017, to October 7, 2017.

PUBLISHED WORKS

Burroughs, Benjamin, Adam Rugg, David Becker, and Madeline Edgmon. "#VegasStrong: Sport, Public Memorialization, and the Golden Knights." *Communication & Sport* 9, no. 1 (February 1, 2021): 110–27. https://doi.org/10.1177/2167479519855085.

Chang, Stewart. "Our National Psychosis: Guns, Terror, and Hegemonic Masculinity." *Harvard Civil Rights—Civil Liberties Law Review* 53, no. 2 (Fall 2018): 495–531.

Erdem, Mehmet, Saeed Hasanzadeh, and Billy Bai. "One October Tragedy in Las Vegas: An Overview of Tourists' Perceptions." *Journal of Tourism, Heritage & Services Marketing* 6, no. 3 (October 2020): 59–63. https://doi.org/10.5281/zenodo.4108431.

Evans, Stefani, and Donna McAleer. *Healing Las Vegas: The Las Vegas Community Healing Garden in Response to the 1 October Tragedy.* Reno: University of Nevada Press, 2019.

Fortini, Amanda. "'I Realized I Was Probably Going to Die There': Surviving the Las Vegas Shooting." *New Yorker,* October 5, 2017. https://www.newyorker.com/news/news-desk/i-realized-i-was-probably-going-to-die-there-surviving-the-las-vegas-shooting.

———. "Life After Near-Death in the Las Vegas Shooting." *New Yorker,* October 29, 2017. https://www.newyorker.com/news/news-desk/life-after-near-death-in-the-las-vegas-shooting.

———. "Op-Ed: One Year After the Las Vegas Shooting: Life Goes on, but Not for Everyone." *Los Angeles Times,* September 30, 2018. https://www.latimes.com/opinion/op-ed/la-oe-fortini-las-vegas-shooting-anniversary-20180930-story.html.

———. "The Funeral Parlor Giving Families Peace After the Las Vegas Shooting." *New Yorker, October 11, 2017.* https://www.newyorker.com/news/news-desk/giving-families-peace-at-a-funeral-parlor-after-the-las-vegas-shooting.

———. "What Happened in Vegas." *California Sunday Magazine,* May 22, 2018. https://story.californiasunday.com/las-vegas-shooting.

Hick, John L., Jessie Nelson, John Fildes, Deborah Kuhls, Alexander Eastman, and David Dries. "Triage, Trauma, and Today's Mass Violence Events." *Journal of the American College of Surgeons* 230, no. 2 (February 1, 2020): 251–56. https://doi.org/10.1016/j.jamcollsurg.2019.10.011.

Kim, Tammi. "Archiving the 1 October Web." History@Work blog, National Council on Public History. April 17, 2018. https://ncph.org/history-at-work/archiving-the-1-october-web/.

Kuhls, Deborah A., John J. Fildes, Matthew Johnson, Sean D. Dort, L. M. Jacobs, Alexander E. Eastman, Robert J. Winchell, and Ronald M. Stewart. "Southern Nevada Trauma System Uses Proven Techniques to Save Lives After 1 October Shooting." *Bulletin of the American College of Surgeons* 103, no. 3 (2018): 39–45.

Lawter, Dylan, and Anya Sanko. "Guns in the Sky: Nevada's Firearm Laws, 1 October, and Next Steps." *Nevada Law Journal Forum* 5, no. 1 (June 21, 2021): 34–70. https://scholars.law.unlv.edu/nljforum/vol5/iss1/4.

Mazmanyan, Kelsey. "Student Perceptions of the Library During Times of Terror: Exploratory Research Surveying Students Affected by the October 1 Shooting and Their Impressions of Safety in the Academic Library Community." *College and Research Libraries* 81, no. 1 (January 1, 2020): 109–21. https://doi.org/10.5860/crl.81.1 .109.

Quinn, Jeffrey S. "#VegasStrong, One Year Later." *Health Security* 16, no. 5 (October 1, 2018): 350–55. https://doi.org/10.1089/hs.2018.0084.

Thompson, D. S., T. Marshall, L. R. Bali, I. Chung, and D. Slattery. "Change in Emergency Department Volume Following the Las Vegas October Shooting." *Annals of Emergency Medicine,* Abstracts, 74, no. 4, Supplement (October 1, 2019): S53. https://doi.org/10.1016/j.annemergmed.2019.08.137.

Presentations in Digital Scholarship at UNLV

https://digitalscholarship.unlv.edu/one_oct_presentations/.

Blankenship, Mary. "How Misinformation Spreads Through Twitter." In *Brookings Minor Culminating Projects,* 2020. https://digitalscholarship.unlv.edu/brookings _capstone_studentpapers/6.

Knapp, Kaitlin, and Briona Haney. "Studio G Special Report Nov. 2, 2017." UNLV *1 October Presentations & Events,* November 2, 2017. https://digitalscholarship.unlv .edu/one_oct_presentations/4.

Sabbath, Roberta. "Archiving the 1 October 2017 Las Vegas Tragedy: Social Media as Greek Chorus." *Lectures/Events,* July 30, 2018. https://digitalscholarship.unlv.edu /english_lectures_events/14.

Sabbath, Roberta, Stefani Evans, Eryn Green, and Dan Bubb. "Bearing Witness in a Human City: The 1 October 2017 Las Vegas Mass Shooting." UNLV *1 October Presentations & Events,* November 14, 2021. https://digitalscholarship.unlv.edu/one_oct _presentations/3.

UNLV TV, University of Nevada, Las Vegas. "1 October Remembrance Ceremony." UNLV *1 October Presentations & Events,* October 1, 2018. https://digitalscholarship .unlv.edu/one_oct_presentations/2.

Contributors

DANIEL BUBB is an associate professor in residence at the University of Nevada, Las Vegas, Honors College. He received his MA in history from UNLV and his interdisciplinary PhD in history and political science from the University of Missouri, Kansas City. He is a former commercial pilot who has published articles on commercial aviation and airport histories in a variety of academic journals and magazines. His book *Landing in Las Vegas: Commercial Aviation and the Making of a Tourist City* is available from the University of Nevada Press.

SU KIM CHUNG is head of public services at the University of Nevada, Las Vegas, Libraries Special Collections and Archives, where she oversees reference, instruction, and outreach. She is also curator of entertainment, LGBTQ, and women's history collections.

STEFANI EVANS is an oral historian and project manager at the Oral History Research Center at University Libraries, University of Nevada, Las Vegas. Evans co-edited *Healing Las Vegas: The Las Vegas Community Healing Garden in Response to the 1 October Tragedy,* published by the University of Nevada Press, which draws from about seventy oral histories of 1 October and hundreds of photographs of the garden.

PRISCILLA FINLEY is the humanities librarian at the University of Nevada, Las Vegas, Libraries, supporting faculty and students in the departments of history, English, philosophy, world languages and cultures, theater and film.

CAROLYN GOODMAN, longtime resident of Las Vegas, is the founder, president, and trustee emeritus of the *Meadows School*. She has been elected mayor of Las Vegas three times, most recently in April 2019, with 83.5 percent of the vote.

ERYN GREEN is an assistant professor in residence in the Department of English at the University of Nevada, Las Vegas, where he serves as coordinator for the World Literature Program. His award-winning works have been featured in *New York Times, Bennington Review, Columbia Review,* and elsewhere.

Terri Keener is a licensed clinical social worker with more than thirty years of professional experience working with populations affected by trauma in various communities and settings. She is the behavioral health coordinator at the Vegas Strong Resiliency Center, which serves those who were affected by the Route 91 Harvest Festival shooting.

Laurie Lytel received her MSW from the University of Michigan and LCSW from the State of Nevada. She has been a practicing psychotherapist for more than thirty years, working with children, adolescents, and families. She also teaches part-time at the School of Social Work at the Greenspun College of Urban Affairs at the University of Nevada, Las Vegas, and has volunteered for the Vegas Strong Resiliency Center since its inception.

AC Monrroy grew up in rural Nevada and received a BA in criminal justice from the University of Nevada, Las Vegas. She was a Housing and Residential Life coordinator for the Dayton Complex residence hall at UNLV at the time of the shooting and is now assistant director for Student Conduct and Safety in the Residential Life, Housing and Food Service Department at the University of Nevada, Reno. She earned her master's degree in higher education administration from the University of Kansas and came back to Nevada to renew her Nevada System of Higher Education journey.

Tennille Pereira is a Las Vegas attorney with the Legal Aid Center of Southern Nevada. When 1 October happened, she facilitated and provided civil legal services for the bereaved families and survivors of the shooting. She eventually became the director of the Vegas Strong Resiliency Center, was appointed to the 1 October Memorial Committee by Governor Steve Sisolak, and later was elected as chairwoman of the committee.

Ashley Primack is a survivor of the Route 91 Harvest Festival tragedy from Las Vegas. She graduated from the University of Nevada, Reno, majoring in psychology and minoring in human development and family studies. She aspires to earn a juris doctor degree after graduating with her bachelor's degree.

Roberta Sabbath is a University of Nevada, Las Vegas, religious studies director and visiting assistant professor in the Department of English, where she teaches Bible as literature, mythology, and world literature. Active in the religious studies field, Sabbath serves in leadership roles, presents at conferences, and publishes in a variety of formats.

CYNTHIA SANFORD has an MA in anthropology and more than twenty years of experience working in museum collections management at local history museums and for the US Holocaust Memorial Museum. She is the registrar at the Clark County Museum in Henderson, where she manages more than one million objects, including the *Remembering 1 October Collection,* consisting of items left at memorials to victims of the mass shooting.

MYNDA SMITH was born and raised in Salt Lake City, Utah, and moved to Las Vegas more than twenty-five years ago. Tragically, her only sister, Neysa Tonks, was one of the fifty-eight victims of the October 1, 2017, mass shooting. Smith is a dedicated member of the 1 October Memorial Committee.

BARBARA TABACH has been a longtime Las Vegas oral historian. She is the project director of *Veterans' Voices: An Oral History Project,* which partners with the Women's Research Center of Nevada and the Military and Veteran Service Center at the University of Nevada, Las Vegas. Previously, Tabach worked as an oral historian and project manager for the Lied Library's Oral History Research Center at UNLV. Her contributions are included in *Remembering 1 October, Southern Nevada Jewish Heritage Project, Latinx Voices of Southern Nevada,* and others.

DINA TITUS is the first congressional district representative of Nevada. She has also served as a representative of seventh district in the Nevada State Senate, and she was minority leader until 2008. Titus was a University of Nevada, Las Vegas, political science professor for thirty-four years until retiring in 2011.

CLAYTEE D. WHITE is working on projects that include Latinx voices, Asian American Pacific Islanders, and the African American experience in Las Vegas. She hosts and moderates televised episodes of *We Need to Talk,* a series designed to address systemic racism in all its manifestations.

Index